"YOUR FAITH HAS MADE YOU WELL"

Renay and Jack,

"YOUR FAITH HAS MADE YOU WELL"

JESUS HEALS IN THE NEW TESTAMENT

I'm so glad our paths have crossed.
God bless you and yours with all good—
Barbara Hosbach

BARBARA HOSBACH

Paulist Press
New York / Mahwah, NJ

Cover image by Lars Justinen / Goodsalt.com
Cover and book design by Lynn Else

Library of Congress Cataloging-in-Publication Data

Hosbach, Barbara.
    Your faith has made you well : Jesus heals in the New Testament / Barbara Hosbach.
        pages cm
    ISBN 978-0-8091-4888-2 (pbk. : alk. paper) — ISBN 978-1-58768-395-4 (ebook)
    1. Bible. Gospels—Criticism, interpretation, etc. 2. Healing in the Bible. 3. Healing—Biblical teaching. 4. Miracles—Biblical teaching. 5. Jesus Christ. I. Title.
    BS2555.6.H4H67 2014
    226.7´06—dc23

                                                            2014016537

ISBN 978-0-8091-4888-2 (paperback)
ISBN 978-1-58768-395-4 (e-book)

Published by Paulist Press
997 Macarthur Boulevard
Mahwah, New Jersey 07430

www.paulistpress.com

Printed and bound in the
United States of America

In loving memory of
Jacqueline Lis and Karen Riley

Contents

Acknowledgments

I would like to thank my husband, Ray Hosbach, and my sister, Marie Ruszkay, for their encouragement and for reading the first draft of this book and providing honest feedback. I also want to thank fellow writer Karen Kelly Boyce for her supportive and helpful suggestions. Thanks too to my editor, Lisa Biedenbach, and to all the people at Paulist Press for their interest, guidance, and efforts in bringing this project to publication.

Introduction

> There is not much profit in just thinking, "Wow, Jesus worked another miracle!" But there is much profit in noting the changed status, self-image, courage, and relationship to family or community that the cure invariably entails. This is the real transformative message.
>
> Richard Rohr, adapted from *The Four Gospels*

Although most of us may not be blind, deaf, or crippled physically, we might find ourselves blinded by denial. How many of us are deaf to things we don't want to hear or to the needs of others, in society or even under our own roofs? How many of us are crippled by depression, anxiety, or any number of challenges not apparent to the naked eye?

Health involves so much more than the absence of physical problems. Those Jesus did heal physically were invited to further healing, to become well not only in body but also in mind and spirit: a holistic approach, as we might say today. Jesus invited the woman healed of hemorrhaging to face him honestly rather than slink away unnoticed. He forgave the sins of the paralytic before healing the man's paralysis. Some healings weren't on the physical level at all, such as the woman who anointed Jesus and, through her encounter with him, was healed of shame.

"Your Faith Has Made You Well" explores accounts of Jesus' healing ministry taken from all four Gospels. This collection of

stories makes clear that there was no one-size-fits-all healing method. Healings were as varied as the people seeking them. Jesus responded to different needs and circumstances in a number of ways. While many people sought him out, some were brought to him by others. In still other cases, Jesus initiated the healing on his own. Sometimes he simply gave a command, and with a word the sufferer was healed. Some people he touched, laying hands on them or using his own saliva as an instrument of healing. At times Jesus even healed people not physically present, as with the Roman officer's servant. One blind man required a second treatment before he was able to see clearly. In another case, Jesus covered the eyes of a blind man with mud, blocking the man's vision even more. This required him to go and wash; once he did, his eyesight was restored. Sometimes things have to get worse before they get better.

Jesus' healing power speaks to all of us who are willing to turn to him and have our eyes, ears, minds, and hearts opened to what he offers us. Each chapter of this book begins with the Scripture account of a healing story and then takes a deeper look at what happened during the process. Chapters explore what those encounters might have felt like when viewed through the eyes of the people involved. Questions at the end of each chapter—which can be used for private reflection or group discussion—invite readers to identify with each story in a personal way and explore its relevance now. A brief prayer completes each chapter's reflection.

While we may not have the charism to heal others physically, all of us can cooperate with God's desire for our wholeness in body, mind, and spirit. We can use our talents and abilities to minister to others by listening, serving, or sharing our own hope and experience with the healing power of God's love.

With *"Your Faith Has Made You Well"* I invite you to relate to the biblical accounts of Jesus' healing in a deeper way and to consider what they have to say to you and to those around you who may be in need of healing today.

Be of good faith. Be well.

The Man with an Unclean Spirit

Evil in a Holy Place

[Jesus] went down to Capernaum, a city in Galilee, and was teaching them on the sabbath. They were astounded at his teaching, because he spoke with authority. In the synagogue there was a man who had the spirit of an unclean demon, and he cried out with a loud voice, "Let us alone! What have you to do with us, Jesus of Nazareth? Have you come to destroy us? I know who you are, the Holy One of God." But Jesus rebuked him, saying, "Be silent, and come out of him!" When the demon had thrown him down before them, he came out of him without having done him any harm. They were all amazed and kept saying to one another, "What kind of utterance is this? For with authority and power he commands the unclean spirits, and out they come!"

Luke 4:31–36

The man came to a place of worship even though he had a spirit of evil within him. Interestingly, the evil spirit could not override the man's free will nor keep him from entering the holy place to hear God's word. Even so, simply hearing the word of God was not enough to eradicate the spirit from the man's heart. Unlike others who recounted Scripture, Jesus taught with "authority" (Matt 7:28). Jesus' authoritative pronouncement of truth made evil uncomfortable enough to cry out. And what did it cry out? "Let us alone!" The evil spirit knew Jesus was not only holy but *the* Holy One. It had the power to influence others to make poor use of their free will, but it knew God's power was greater.

Perhaps the man only ventured to the synagogue because he knew Jesus would be there. On the other hand, maybe the man had been attending weekly services for years, with little or no effect. Maybe he'd simply never been uncomfortable enough to change until he encountered Jesus. Because this encounter took place very early in Jesus' ministry, it's quite possible the man had never heard of Jesus before. In fact, we're told that Jesus' fame began to spread "at once" after he cast out this unclean spirit (Mark 1:21–28).

THE DISTURBING TRUTH

In any event, the evil spirit cried out, asking to be left alone. So often, temptations beg to be left alone. As St. Augustine prayed, "Lord, grant me chastity…but not yet." We *want* to stop indulging in ways that damage our health, our self-esteem, or our pocket-books—but not if we have to give up the treats we like. We *long* to have better relationships—but not if we have to do the hard work of looking within and searching out how we contribute to the unhealthy patterns. When loved ones suggest we need to make changes or get help, we cry out, "I'll handle it myself," which may mean we don't want to handle it at all. The self-destructive seductions within our hearts just want to be left alone.

Jesus' truth made the spirit uncomfortable enough to cry out. Sometimes we're uncomfortable when we glimpse what we could be. We go along with the crowd and tolerate the status quo of our poor choices. Then, some moment of truth shows us the finer things we're capable of. For example, one victim of the Columbine shooting was asked if she believed in God. She had the courage of her convictions and answered "yes." Her assailant had the power to pull the trigger but not the power to make the young victim renounce her belief. There are times when we must acknowledge the truth, at least to ourselves. In those moments, will we choose to listen to our Higher Power or some lower power?

And so it was with this man. The spirit within him could not coexist in the presence of holiness. The evil spirit said, "What have you to do with us, Jesus of Nazareth?" There is no common ground. We're told that we can be forgiven for any evil choice we may make—except speaking against the Holy Spirit (Matt 12:31–32). The spirit of holiness has nothing to do with the spirit of evil. God loves us no matter what we do, but because he loves us, he can't pretend evil is acceptable. He invites us to something better.

POSSESSION AND FREE WILL

Jesus ordered the spirit to stop talking and leave the man. It seems strange, in our culture, to think of a demon possessing us, as if we are invaded by a separate entity. But what about an alcoholic who does not want to drink and picks up a drink anyway? Or a mother who promises herself not to scream at her child but screams anyway? As many of us have probably done, St. Paul cried out, "For I do not do the good I want, but the evil I do not want is what I do. Now if I do what I do not want, it is no longer I that do it, but sin that dwells within me" (Rom 7:19–20). Paul goes on to say that he sees his body at war with the law that his mind accepts as good. He calls himself a "wretched man" and asks who will rescue him. Then he answers himself by saying, "Thanks be to God through Jesus Christ our Lord!" (Rom 7:24–25).

Cartoon images of an angel and devil on opposing shoulders are not accurate. Jesus is always bigger than any self-destructive voice. Just as Jesus told the demon to be quiet, we, who have the Holy Spirit within us, can choose to turn a deaf ear to the seductive voices. We don't do this on our own but by the power of the Holy Spirit and those agents of God's grace that God puts in our path.

The unclean spirit did leave the man, but first it threw him down before the other witnesses. In Mark's Gospel, the spirit convulsed the man and cried out in a loud voice. Sometimes we too don't let go of a self-destructive habit without kicking and screaming. It's uncomfortable. It can even hurt. We may have to be humbled, perhaps in front of other witnesses, as we confront our demons. We may have to get thrown down to our knees before we're willing to let those demons go. It's okay. We don't have to be afraid of the discomfort. The spirit threw the man down but left "without having done him any harm." Feeling uncomfortable is not the same as being damaged. Think of a mother in labor: not all pain leads to destruction.

In spite of his discomfort, the man was willing to let the evil within him go. Although Jesus ordered the demon to come out, Jesus did not heal the man against his will. Jesus would never take away the gift of free will given by his Father. Jesus will always free us of our demons, if we are willing to let them go.

PONDER

1. What do you think drew the man to the synagogue in spite of the fact that he had an evil spirit within him?

2. What challenges might the man have experienced during his encounter with Jesus?

3. Like St. Paul, when have you observed yourself doing something you did not want to do? What happened?

4. When you or someone you care about wrestles with inner demons, in what ways can you turn to God and appropriate God's healing power?

PRAY

Loving Savior, my self-destructive tendencies want to be left alone. Remind me that you are greater than my demons. It is safe to surrender myself to your care.

2

Simon Peter's Mother-in-Law

Lifting Our Spirits

As soon as they left the synagogue, they entered the house of Simon and Andrew, with James and John. Now Simon's mother-in-law was in bed with a fever, and they told [Jesus] about her at once. He came and took her by the hand and lifted her up. Then the fever left her, and she began to serve them. That evening at sundown, they brought to him all who were sick or possessed with demons. And the whole city was gathered around the door. And he cured many who were sick with various diseases, and cast out many demons; and he would not permit the demons to speak, because they knew him.

Mark 1:29–34

Jesus had just miraculously healed a man with an evil spirit. Straight from the synagogue, Jesus and his followers went to Simon's house. Although the word must have spread like wildfire, the townspeople didn't bring the sick to Jesus until sundown. That's because this all happened on the Sabbath. The people believed it was against the law to heal on the Sabbath.

Healing was considered work, and the Sabbath was a day of rest, which didn't end until sunset.

The people who had seen or heard about the miracle must have trusted Jesus' power to heal. Evidently that trust wasn't strong enough to overcome the religious constraints that had crystallized over the years. Longing for healing, they sought the power that went beyond the established religion. Still, they were unwilling or unable to give up the security that establishment seemed to offer. Obeying the Sabbath law did not protect people from sickness or from unclean spirits. Nevertheless, they seemed unable to grasp that Jesus' power could do more than heal their bodies; it could also free them from the burden of what Sabbath rest had come to mean. So they waited for sundown.

LIFTED UP

In contrast, Jesus' close followers didn't hesitate. They told him "at once" about Simon's sick mother-in-law. They had seen and trusted not only Jesus' power but also his holiness and authority. Jesus didn't hesitate either but responded immediately. He took the sick woman by the hand, lifted her up, and the fever left her.

How often are we lifted up by the presence of someone who reaches out to us in our suffering? Sometimes lifting our spirits can be just as important as physical recovery. So often we can't raise ourselves up out of our own pain. It's easy for our morale to sink to the depths when our bodies hurt or our brains are fevered by anxious thoughts. In isolation there may be nothing to interrupt our focus on how miserable we feel. When we can't see beyond the horizon of our own distress, sometimes others can help us shift our focus. Whether or not they realize it, they then become channels of God's healing love.

After Jesus touched and lifted up the suffering woman, she

had a higher vantage point than when she was flat on her back. What did she do once that happened? She began to serve others.

We aren't told how long Simon's mother-in-law had lain in bed before Jesus encountered her. When we're sick, there's certainly a time to rest and allow healing to take place. We need to let others minister to us, as Peter's mother-in-law allowed Jesus to help her. There are times when pushing ourselves doesn't help anyone. But it's also true that there's something very healing about being of service to others. When we think about another person's needs besides our own, it can be healing for us, too. Shifting focus from our cares and worries can help shrink them to their proper proportion. Simple but genuine service (rather than compulsive martyrdom) can bless us with freedom from self-centeredness. It also brings a sense of usefulness that encourages healthy self-esteem and the self-confidence that comes from using our talents to help others.

RESPONDING IN SERVICE

Just as the disciples told Jesus about Simon's mother-in-law's sickness at once and he healed her at once, she also began to wait on them at once. Luke's version of the story says that she "immediately" got up and began to serve them. I don't know what the Sabbath laws say about women's work. Perhaps Simon's mother-in-law only served others in ways permitted on the Sabbath, or maybe, having been healed on the Sabbath, she did not feel constrained to limit her service. Either way, she immediately felt free to help those around her.

Any healing we may experience is, of course, very welcome. However, if it doesn't lead us beyond ourselves to helping others, as we are able to, our healing may not be complete. Because of their limitations, some people may never be what society thinks of as productive. That's okay. Being helpful and being productive are two different things. A welcoming smile, a kind word, or a look of appreciation may be just the boost needed to lift someone else's spirit. The disciples didn't wait. Jesus didn't wait. Simon's mother-in-law didn't wait. If there is something we can do today, to reach out to someone who's hurting or who needs what we have to offer, why wait? There's no time like the present.

PONDER

1. The fever left Simon's mother-in-law when Jesus touched her and lifted her up. When have you been touched and lifted up from feverish thoughts or activity? What happened?
2. The people who waited until sunset to bring the sick for healing weren't wrong, but they may have suffered longer than was necessary. In what ways has your own healing been delayed?
3. What role does trust play in the healing process?
4. How do you know when to rest and nurture yourself and when to help others?
5. Once healed, Simon's mother-in-law began to serve others. From what do you need to be healed in order to be able to serve others better?

PRAY

Lord, when I can't see beyond my own pain and anxiety, lift me up. Teach me to lift others up by reaching out as a channel of your healing love.

3

Four Fishermen

Vocational Healing

Once while Jesus was standing beside the lake of Gennesaret, and the crowd was pressing in on him to hear the word of God, he saw two boats there at the shore of the lake; the fishermen had gone out of them and were washing their nets. He got into one of the boats, the one belonging to Simon, and asked him to put out a little way from the shore. Then he sat down and taught the crowds from the boat. When he had finished speaking, he said to Simon, "Put out into the deep water and let down your nets for a catch." Simon answered, "Master, we have worked all night long but have caught nothing. Yet if you say so, I will let down the nets." When they had done this, they caught so many fish that their nets were beginning to break. So they signaled their partners in the other boat to come and help them. And they came and filled both boats, so that they began to sink. But when Simon Peter saw it, he fell down at Jesus' knees, saying, "Go away from me, Lord, for I am a sinful man!" For he and all who were with him were amazed at the catch of fish that they had taken; and so also were James and John, sons of Zebedee, who were partners with Simon. Then Jesus said to Simon, "Do not be afraid; from now on you will be catching people." When they had brought their boats to shore, they left everything and followed him.

Luke 5:1–11

Four experienced fishermen worked all night but didn't catch a thing. All their skill and training couldn't make the fish bite. They had the good sense to call it a day and were washing their nets when Jesus called them.

Jesus eased them into a change of vocation that started with a practical need. The crowd pressing in on Jesus backed him up against the water's edge. He needed a little space to be able to teach the crowd without being overwhelmed by them. The fishermen just happened to be docked—perhaps earlier than usual because their work had been unsuccessful. They were available when Jesus needed them. What he asked them to do wasn't all that demanding. Allowing him to sit in their boat a short distance from shore didn't ask more of them than they could deliver. Even though they must have been tired and perhaps demoralized after working all night with no results, Simon Peter and his brother Andrew helped Jesus. They allowed him into their boat, so that Jesus could safely continue teaching.

When Jesus was finished with the task at hand, he told Simon to go out fishing again. What did a carpenter know about fishing? Simon, the professional, explained why that wasn't a reasonable thing to do, but he deferred to Jesus. Maybe what he heard Jesus say to the crowd convinced him to obey Jesus. With nothing more to go on than trust in Jesus, Simon and Andrew went into "the deep water" and tried again. This time their efforts were so successful that they called their partners who willingly helped haul in the miraculous catch.

The abundant results more than repaid Simon Peter and

his brother Andrew for the use of their boat. It demonstrated that Jesus offered dynamic faith in action as well as words of wisdom. Awed by the light of Jesus' holy power, Peter became well aware of his own human failings. In contrast to Jesus, Peter's own unworthiness must have been painfully clear. No wonder he thought Jesus should go away.

But Jesus wasn't looking for perfection. He was looking for people open to his message and willing to follow him. Step by step, Peter and his friends all demonstrated their willingness to act on Jesus' prompting.

A STEP-BY-STEP CALLING

Initially, Jesus had called the fishermen to help in a small, not very risky way, and they complied. By allowing Jesus to use their boat, the men were exposed to his teaching in a nonthreatening way. Then Jesus invited them to get more involved by putting out into "deep water." Against logic, the fishermen again complied and were astonished by the rewarding results. Peter voiced what the others may have felt—their own unworthiness to receive such a staggering gift. Who were they to associate with a giver whose generosity and power was so overwhelming? Jesus reassured Simon and the rest, telling them not to be afraid. Fear of their own inadequacies could have kept them from answering their call to serve. Jesus offered healing from that fear. Only then did he reveal his ultimate purpose for them: he invited them to follow him and start "catching people."

One has to wonder what was involved in their willingness to abandon the familiar and change careers. Was it just the one long night of fishing and coming up empty or had there been a string of such nights? Had thoughts of packing in the fishing business come up for a while or were they in a business-as-usual frame of mind when Jesus reached out to them? What drew these men to Jesus? Was it the sheer force of the truth they heard in his words spoken from their boat or time spent in close proximity to him? Maybe for each of them—James, John, Andrew, Peter—it was some different combination of all these factors.

HEALING FROM FEAR OF INADEQUACY

It's easy to see why the fishermen felt their own inadequacy being in Jesus' presence, let alone helping him carry out his mission. Maybe we feel the same way and ask: "Who am I? I'm not so holy. Serving the Body of Christ is for those who are up to it: priests, religious brothers and sisters, pious people. I'll never be up for canonization. I'm just a regular person." Well, who could be more regular, more down-to-earth, than a bunch of fishermen? Sailors are not known for their Sunday-school speech or polished manners, and yet these four were at the heart of Jesus' ministry. Who better to speak to regular people than regular people?

We shouldn't let our inclinations toward humility mislead us into thinking we have nothing to offer. Like the four fishermen, all we really need is willingness and openness to follow Jesus' instructions.

We don't have to hold back out of fear. As Jesus invited Peter and the others, he probably won't overwhelm us at first. His promptings might start off subtly without demanding too much from us. We can simply take the first simple step that is in front of us to act in service. Once we do, we may find it isn't as challenging as we might have feared. We may even become comfortable. Based on that experience, we might become willing to move into "deeper water." Step by step, we can be drawn into God's plan for our lives with no fear about our inadequacy for the task at hand. If the Lord calls us, it's because he knows we are the ones who can do what he has in mind for us to do. It might be that no one else could do it in quite the same way. We can be assured that the results of our efforts will turn out the way God has in mind for them to turn out. That's true whether our efforts any given day result in an overwhelming yield or apparently none at all. In fact, an unsuccessful venture might just make us available for the next opportunity God has in mind for us.

PONDER

1. Even though Peter and the others fished all night without success, they were right where they needed to be to answer Jesus' call. When have your best efforts gotten you nowhere? How might that have put you in a position to be better able to serve?

2. Why do you think Peter was willing to put into deeper water even though his professional experience made the prospect unlikely to be effective? When have you been willing to put into deeper water knowing that the desired result might not be achieved?

3. Once Peter witnessed the miraculous catch, he became aware of his own inadequacies. That made him uncomfortable in Jesus' presence. How comfortable are you with bringing your own inadequacies to God?

4. After their encounter with Jesus, all four fishermen "left everything and followed" Jesus. What do you need to leave behind in order to follow Jesus more closely?

PRAY

My Creator, you know me better than I know myself. Self-doubt can keep me from responding to your call. Reassure me that you provide everything I need to follow you.

4

The Leper

Restored to Community Life

A leper came to [Jesus] begging him, and kneeling he said to him, "If you choose, you can make me clean." Moved with pity, Jesus stretched out his hand and touched him, and said to him, "I do choose. Be made clean!" Immediately the leprosy left him, and he was made clean. After sternly warning him he sent him away at once, saying to him, "See that you say nothing to anyone; but go, show yourself to the priest, and offer for your cleansing what Moses commanded, as a testimony to them." But he went out and began to proclaim it freely, and to spread the word, so that Jesus could no longer go into a town openly, but stayed out in the country; and people came to him from every quarter.

Mark 1:40–45

The leper dared to approach Jesus even though it was forbidden. Once determined "unclean" by the priests, lepers had to live outside the camp, wear torn clothes, and leave their hair uncombed. As if that wasn't enough to keep others away, they had to call out, "Unclean, unclean!" to make sure people kept their distance (Lev

13:45–46). What a lonely, miserable way to live! It's bad enough to be isolated, but forced to wear rags and give up personal grooming? That's adding insult to injury, literally.

No wonder the leper begged for Jesus' help. Kneeling in a position of respect, he made his request: if you want to, Jesus, you can heal me. It's up to you. The beggar audaciously approached Jesus while respecting Jesus' right to choose whether or not to heal him. Audacity and humility are an interesting combination. That might be a sincere testimony to the man's faith.

Jesus was moved with pity. Of course he wanted to help the man. Why would Jesus ever choose *not* to heal? How could healing *not* be Jesus' will for us? We're told that Jesus was unable to perform many miracles in his hometown because the people did not have faith (Mark 6:5–6). Maybe those people were too familiar with Jesus to respect his power. It's unfortunate but understandable. It reminds me of when I used to swim at the local Y almost daily. One day I hesitated because it was the first time that the lifeguard on duty was my daughter's fifteen-year-old friend. *I babysat for her just a few years ago*, I thought. *And now my life is in her hands?* It felt strange to entrust myself to someone who once needed my care. Since the leper had no prior experience of Jesus being anything but a healer, nothing blocked his confidence in Jesus' power to heal. He trusted Jesus enough to break social barriers.

Even so, I resist the idea that if people aren't healed, it's their own fault because they lack faith. A close friend—one of the most faith-filled people I've ever met—is wheelchair-bound due to multiple sclerosis. She shared her devastation with me after someone criticized her for lacking the faith that would enable her to walk. Blaming people for physical challenges doesn't contribute to the healing process. It can leave them feeling even more isolated. Faith is not a commodity that we can conjure up by force of unaided will. Ironically, faith is sometimes demonstrated by accepting our crosses and choosing to follow Jesus when life isn't the way we would like it to be. In spite of illness, good can be done.

Having heard the good news about Jesus, the leper believed in Jesus' power but did not demand healing or presume it was Jesus' will. Instead, the leper entrusted himself to the care of whatever Jesus' will for him might have been. That's a testimony of even deeper faith. We can trust not only God's power but also that God's will is for our greatest good, whether or not that includes physical healing.

RESTORED TO COMMUNITY LIFE

After healing the man, Jesus instructed him not to tell anyone but to go to the priest and offer the customary sacrifice. This verification of his cure would have marked the man's return to his community. He had been healed in an extraordinary way, but his healing was not complete until the man was reunited with those he'd been cut off from. Although participating in the prescribed healing rubrics would have accomplished this, the man broke his isolation by spreading the word of what Jesus had done for him. Contrary to his instructions, the leper spread the word about his healing so much that it affected Jesus' ability to travel. I suppose it's forgivable that the man shouted his good news from the housetops. Maybe it was a bit much to expect that anyone could keep such an astonishing miracle to himself—especially someone who'd been cut off from people for who knows how long. From outcast to celebrity status instantaneously, it's easy to see how he got carried away. Who wouldn't have shared the news with everybody he came in contact with?

SELF-IMPOSED QUARANTINE

What does this man's story have to do with us? Some of us have been isolated due to poor health or because of economic, educational, or other social barriers. Others, who march to the beat of a different drummer, may have felt like square pegs in round holes ever since childhood. Many of us choose to isolate ourselves when we're having a rough time for any number of reasons. We voluntarily treat ourselves much like the leper. We stay home in dirty pajamas or a ratty bathrobe and pull the covers over our heads. We don't shower or comb our hair. We transmit the message loud and clear that we want to be alone. We determine that we are unclean, unfit for the company of others. The spiral of isolation continues in its downward trajectory every time we look in the mirror.

We don't share our problems because we fear others will reject us. Instead, we beat them to the punch and reject ourselves. If we aren't up to putting our best foot forward, we may not feel emotionally healthy enough to be around others at all. We deny ourselves the healing opportunity of unconditional love, the gift of being accepted just as we are. Our friends, loved ones, or even professionals may not have the power to heal us of our troubles instantly. What others can do is help us break out of the self-imposed isolation that makes the problems we're struggling with loom larger.

People with skin diseases can't really cover them up. Their condition is out in the open for all to see. Unlike them, we can choose to cover up our inner blemishes and sore spots, hoping no one else will see, but what does that gain us? We are as alone as if we were in quarantine. There's a saying that we're only as sick as our secrets. Granted, we don't have to broadcast our difficulties in public. Discretion is always wise, but discretion is not the same as going it alone. Surely God will lead us to at least one trusted person we can share our challenges with honestly and confidentially, be it a friend, loved one, or professional. God's wisdom is a powerful, sustaining source of guidance for us all, no matter what keeps us from the fullness of life. We can start by praying for a balance of hope, trust, awe, and enough healthy self-love to take the risk.

PONDER

1. The leper asked Jesus to make him well. He trusted Jesus' ability but did not presume Jesus' response. What's the difference between a hopeful request and an expectation?
2. What isolates you from others? What would it take to be healed of this isolation?
3. Jesus ordered the healed man to follow the customary procedure for those who had been healed of a skin disease. How does the following of established social procedures counteract a sense of isolation? Is it possible to follow social customs and still remain true to yourself? Why or why not?
4. Once healed, the man could not keep the good news to himself. When have you found it easier to interact with others when you were happy and to isolate yourself from them when you were hurting?

PRAY

Trinity of Love, we're called to live in community. Melt the barriers of fear and pride that isolate me from others.

5

The Paralyzed Man

Standing Upright with God

When [Jesus] returned to Capernaum after some days, it was reported that he was at home. So many gathered around that there was no longer room for them, not even in front of the door; and he was speaking the word to them. Then some people came, bringing to him a paralyzed man, carried by four of them. And when they could not bring him to Jesus because of the crowd, they removed the roof above him; and after having dug through it, they let down the mat on which the paralytic lay. When Jesus saw their faith, he said to the paralytic, "Son, your sins are forgiven." Now some of the scribes were sitting there, questioning in their hearts, "Why does this fellow speak in this way? It is blasphemy! Who can forgive sins but God alone?" At once Jesus perceived in his spirit that they were discussing these questions among themselves; and he said to them, "Why do you raise such questions in your hearts? Which is easier, to say to the paralytic, 'Your sins are forgiven,' or to say, 'Stand up and take your mat and walk?' But so that you may know that the Son of Man has authority on earth to forgive sins"—he said to the paralytic—"I say to you, stand up, take your mat and go to your home." And he stood up, and immediately took the mat and went out before all of them; so that they were all amazed and glorified God, saying, "We have never seen anything like this!"

Mark 2:1–12

I wonder how the paralytic felt when his friends were taking apart the roof. Did he want to get to Jesus at any cost? Maybe the whole thing was his idea. But how might he have felt while he was being lowered down through the ceiling into the middle of the crowd? Talk about making an entrance! Every eye must have been glued on him. How embarrassing! Who was he to steal the attention away from Jesus? What if the poor man never meant for his friends to make a fuss? When he found out it was too crowded to get through the door, maybe he would have preferred not to be healed rather than cause a commotion. Maybe his friends wanted better for him than he wanted for himself, and his embarrassment was a price they were willing to pay. What could he do about it?

There he was, with no possible means of escape—the center of attention, making a circus-type entrance, interrupting whatever wisdom Jesus had been sharing with the crowd. There he was, lying unable to move while every eye in the place burned into him. And just when he thought he couldn't feel any more self-conscious, Jesus said, "Son, your sins are forgiven."

Great! He had the spotlight on him and what did Jesus do but remind him of his sins. Sure, we're all sinners, but this man was singled out as Jesus personally forgave him. Everybody else in that crowd was a sinner, too. Why did Jesus single out this man to forgive? The man didn't ask for forgiveness. It was probably pretty obvious to everyone there what kind of healing he and his friends were looking for.

It was evident to Jesus, too, that the man wanted to be healed of his paralysis. But the passage also said that Jesus saw their faith. The Amplified Bible's 1965 translation may provide a clue. According to this expanded translation, Jesus said, "Son, your sins are forgiven [you] and put away—[that is,] the penalty is remitted, the sense of guilt removed, and you are made upright and in right standing with God" (Mark 2:5). Wow! Of course, when our sins are forgiven, it implies the sense of guilt is removed, but the image of being made upright, of being in "right standing" with God, suggests more. It suggests the freedom to literally stand upright after being relieved of whatever weight had been holding the man down for who knows how long. Jesus seemed to perceive that the burden of guilt was holding the man down more than his physical infirmity. Jesus also perceived that the man and his friends had faith enough to accept God's grace. But that's not all Jesus perceived.

SEEING IS BELIEVING

We're told Jesus was aware that some people well-versed in religious law thought Jesus was blaspheming by daring to forgive the man's sins. They were right in thinking only God alone could forgive sins. They were wrong in failing to recognize Jesus was one with the Father. Since seeing is believing, Jesus demonstrated his holy authority by healing the man physically as well.

As soon as Jesus told the man to stand up, pick up his mat, and go home, the man "immediately" hurried out of there. I don't blame him—talk about sticking out like a sore thumb! We can only imagine what the man was feeling. As he felt the strength course through his body, empowering him to walk and allowing his arm to support his mat, he must have been exuberant! Relief at being out of the spotlight may have washed over him, too. Gratitude that he would no longer be forced to burden his loyal friends probably dawned on him a bit later. I wonder how long it took him to realize that he would no longer be a burden to himself. Whatever guilt had tormented or immobilized him—perhaps even making him think he deserved to be paralyzed—no longer had him in its grips. Blessed freedom!

But he wasn't the only one who was healed that day. Yes, his caregivers were healed of their concern for their beloved friend, but the passage ends by saying that all were amazed and glorified God. The word *all* implies that the religious experts who initially thought Jesus was a blasphemer were also included. They now had evidence that the source of Jesus' power was connected to God. They were healed of their skepticism and religiosity.

WHAT PARALYZES US?

Sometimes guilt, remorse, or shame can paralyze us and keep us from living life more fully. We remain in the shadows, hoping not to draw attention to ourselves. We shrink back from doing things that might make us stand out, so we don't use our God-given abilities. Fear of what others might think could keep us from using our talents in situations outside our comfort zone. Fear might hold us back from going the extra mile to help a loved one overcome something they're struggling with. Self-consciousness can prevent us from reaching out to others. We're afraid that what we have to offer might not be good enough. We might fear that if someone knew the "real" us, they'd run the other way. So we remain paralyzed by our own insecurities. Jesus can heal us, too.

PONDER

1. How do you think the paralyzed man felt as he was being lowered from the roof into the middle of the crowd in front of Jesus?

2. Have you ever wanted something so much for yourself or a loved one that you didn't care about public opinion? What happened?

3. When have you been the center of attention? How did you feel? What circumstances might change your feelings?

4. Is it easier to risk the spotlight for your own well-being or for a loved one's well-being? What makes the difference?

5. When has guilt "paralyzed" you? How did you become free of the paralysis?

PRAY

Loving Father, may the guilt, shame, and fear that paralyze me be dissolved in your unconditional love. Empower me to use the abilities you created me to have.

6

The Woman Who Anointed Jesus

Healing from Shame

And a woman in the city, who was a sinner, having learned that [Jesus] was eating in the Pharisee's house, brought an alabaster jar of ointment. She stood behind him at his feet, weeping, and began to bathe his feet with her tears and to dry them with her hair. Then she continued kissing his feet and anointing them with the ointment. Now when the Pharisee who had invited him saw it, he said to himself, "If this man were a prophet, he would have known who and what kind of woman this is who is touching him—that she is a sinner." Jesus spoke up and said to him, "Simon, I have something to say to you." "Teacher," he replied, "Speak." "A certain creditor had two debtors; one owed five hundred denarii, and the other fifty. When they could not pay, he canceled the debts for both of them. Now which of them will love him more?" Simon answered, "I suppose the one for whom he cancelled the greater debt." And Jesus said to him, "You have judged rightly." Then turning toward the woman, he said to Simon, "Do you see this woman? I entered your house; you gave me no water for my feet, but she has bathed my feet with her tears and dried them with her hair. You gave me no kiss, but from the time I came in she has not stopped kissing my feet. You did not anoint my head with oil, but she has anointed my feet with ointment. Therefore, I tell you, her sins, which were many, have been forgiven; hence she has shown great love. But the one to whom little is forgiven, loves little." Then he said to her, "Your sins are forgiven." But those who were at the table with him began to say among themselves, "Who is this who even forgives sins?" And he said to the woman, "Your faith has saved you; go in peace."

Luke 7:37–50

The woman was a sinner. Everyone in town knew it. Most of all, she herself knew it. Simon was a sinner too, but few people in town probably guessed it—least of all himself. He was, after all, a Pharisee. He worked hard to keep the letter of the law and comply with external religious observances. He probably thought he was doing a pretty good job of it. He had no qualms about inviting Jesus to his home for a meal. As Jesus pointed out, however, Simon failed to extend the customary hospitality of the day to Jesus. Perhaps Simon felt generous in opening his home to Jesus and that his invitation alone was more than sufficient. Why else would he neglect giving his guest a welcoming embrace or the customary courtesy of providing water for his dusty feet?

By contrast, the anonymous woman would never have dared to invite Jesus into her own house and risk bringing scandal to the one she obviously revered. She approached him on safe ground at the home of a respected Pharisee. That would in no way demean Jesus' reputation. Although well aware of her own unworthiness, she didn't let that stop her from following what she felt drawn to do. She stayed at Jesus' feet. Perhaps she never intended to wash them with her tears. What if her nearness to him heightened her sense of remorse? Perhaps she shed tears of joy at being close to Jesus without being turned away in disgust. The cleansing tears may have flowed naturally as her eyes beheld not only her own sin and shame but also Jesus' loving acceptance.

He didn't chase her away. Far from it. He allowed her to minister to him. He had no arrogance that would prevent him from accepting love shown by the likes of her. Jesus didn't assign a lowly status to her. Rather, being allowed to kiss his feet may have been all the kindness her heart could hold at that moment. That privilege was enough, more than enough for her.

Respect for the giver is conferred when we accept a gift the way it is offered. The woman had brought expensive perfumed oil, the best she had, a gift she thought worthy of the Christ. The deeper gift was the gift of herself, her sincerity in responding to Jesus' acceptance. The deepest gift was Jesus' gift to her—actually two gifts. The first gift was his acceptance of her exactly as she was, shame and all. The second was a priceless gift she could never have given herself: forgiveness for all that was in her past—the poor choices and misguided attempts to gain fulfillment that led her to overwhelming shame and regret.

The woman didn't trust in her own sense of worthiness. Instead, she trusted in Jesus' love and mercy. That's probably why Jesus sent her on her way in peace, saying her faith had saved her. What was that faith? It was her trust in who Jesus was, not in who she was. She didn't buy forgiveness with expensive perfume. She didn't earn it with her ministrations. She was forgiven and healed because she encountered healing love and responded.

In contrast, Simon the Pharisee and his associates had little need or room in their hearts for love or mercy. They played by the rules and made a good show of it. Their status was based on it. The loving mercy Jesus extended to this woman not only shocked them but also threatened their whole value system.

BEYOND SHAME

Many of us carry the shame of our past with us: short-sighted or selfish choices, embarrassing mistakes, foolish or mean-spirited decisions, and actions that we wouldn't want to become public knowledge. But whether others find out about our shameful secrets or not, we know about them. Much as we would like to be free of them, they sometimes haunt our memories. When they do, we cringe again, replaying the disgraces or humiliations of our past that damage our self-respect. We may even feel shame about our family of origin, or our past ignorance of how to act properly in certain circles. We may no longer be the thoughtless or insensitive version of ourselves that we once were. We may be miles away from our former selves yet still bound by a sense of mortification for who we think we were— or were told we were by others.

To compensate, we try to prove how far removed we are from our past shame. There is nothing wrong with growing beyond our mistakes or regrets. That's what a spiritual journey is about. There's no need to wallow in what was, thereby sacrificing what God has in mind for us to be. Let's be careful, however, not to overcompensate like the Pharisees. We don't have to cling to outward signs of respectability or our own efforts to be—or at least appear—perfect. When we try to combat shame in this way, we risk thinking we don't need God's mercy. If we convince ourselves we're doing pretty well on our own, we risk looking down on others. That cuts us off from the healing power of God's love that we all need. Moving beyond our shame comes from laying our secrets at the feet of the God who loves us as we are and who does for us what we can never do for ourselves.

PONDER

1. The sinful woman obviously felt unworthy because of her sins, but she didn't let that stop her from approaching Jesus. How does shame block you from giving and receiving love?
2. When have you felt remorse or humiliation? What is the difference between these feelings?
3. Jesus allowed the woman to kiss his feet and massage them with perfume. How comfortable are you when others pamper you? How can allowing another person to treat you well be a sign of respect for them as well as for yourself?
4. Although the woman had little to offer someone like Jesus, she brought the finest thing she had. It was a gift no one else brought him. What do you have to give to Jesus that no one else can give?

PRAY

Merciful Redeemer, encouraged by your love, I lay my shameful secrets at your feet, trusting that the gift of my true self is precious to you.

7

The Woman Healed of Hemorrhaging

Worthy of Help

As [Jesus] went, the crowds pressed in on him. Now there was a woman who had been suffering from hemorrhages for twelve years; and though she had spent all she had on physicians, no one could cure her. She came up behind him and touched the fringe of his clothes, and immediately her hemorrhage stopped. Then Jesus asked, "Who touched me?" When all denied it, Peter said, "Master, the crowds surround you and press in on you." But Jesus said, "Someone touched me; for I noticed that power had gone out from me." When the woman saw that she could not remain hidden, she came trembling; and falling down before him she declared in the presence of all the people why she had touched him; and how she had been immediately healed. He said to her, "Daughter, your faith has made you well; go in peace."

Luke 8:42b–48

Jesus was headed to the home of Jairus, a synagogue official, to heal his little girl. A nameless woman who had been bleeding for twelve years made her way through the crowd to get to Jesus. She shouldn't have been in public at all. A woman was considered unclean during her monthly period and for as long as the bleeding continued. Almost everything and everyone she came in contact with during that time was also considered unclean (see Lev 15:19–28).

Twelve years is a long time to feel contaminated. The woman had done everything known in that culture to be healed, spending all her money on doctors to no avail. Desperate times call for desperate measures. Throwing caution to the wind, she broke the cultural norm. By touching Jesus, she risked making him unclean, too. She didn't want to contaminate him. Maybe that's why she only touched the outermost fringe of his clothes. Picture this woman, with a lifetime of social teaching to overcome, wanting to be healed but not wanting to jeopardize Jesus or anybody else. Her condition was embarrassing to say the least. How dare this temporary outcast from society (if twelve years can be called temporary) approach Jesus in her impure state, especially when he was on a mission to help an important religious official?

Although her desire for wholeness drove her to take an action, the woman apparently tried to be healed on the sly, unnoticed by Jesus or the crowd. Embarrassment and fear were probably at work. Once healed, she hoped, no doubt, to slink away unobtrusively. Why make waves or involve anybody else?

Except, of course, Jesus *was* involved. He felt his healing power flow out to someone in need. Being God, he may well have known who had touched him. Gentleman that he was, however, Jesus did not give away the woman's secret or subject her to public shame. By asking, "Who touched me?" he provided an opportunity for her to "come clean" on more than a physical level.

Peter and the others were puzzled by Jesus' question. With a throng crowding around him, it's likely that many had touched him inadvertently. But this woman's touch had been different. It was purposeful and effective in appropriating Jesus' healing power. It's beyond belief that the woman could have stolen healing from Jesus unbeknown to him. God is ever in control. That being said, requests for healing and heartfelt prayers aren't always spoken out loud. This woman's faith in action *was* her prayer, and it was answered.

COMING CLEAN

Jesus evidently felt it was important to acknowledge the healing. Once Jesus made it public, she knew better than to slink away. She came forward, trembling, perhaps in awe of his knowledge of her. The woman may have feared Jesus' anger, wondering if she had contaminated him, stolen his grace without permission, or hindered him on his mission to help Jairus's daughter. She may have trembled in shame at having mingled with the crowd in her state. Ironically, she had been too humble to stand in front of him and request healing. She barely felt worthy to approach his back. But once the truth was out in the open, she fell down before him. She presented an interesting posture— humbly, on her knees, and yet with the dignity of facing Jesus rather than having to literally sneak behind his back.

Jesus was kind and reassuring when she admitted her truth in front of witnesses. He warmly called her "Daughter." By saying "Your faith has made you well," Jesus did not imply that her unaided faith achieved her cure. After all, she had needed to connect with him before she was healed. Faith in its own right does not confer power on us. Having faith enables us to seek and receive God's power and accept whatever God's plan for us may be. The woman had spoken the truth about her experience and had been accepted. She was able to walk through the crowd on her way home with her head held high, instead of slinking away into obscurity. Jesus was able to tell her to go in peace, reassured that she was well emotionally as well as physically.

WORTHY OF HELP

We are sometimes like this woman in our quest for healing. We feel unworthy of asking for help. Maybe we prefer not to have our troubles—whatever they might be—made known to others. We don't want to be embarrassed or judged. We don't want to risk rejection. We try self-help projects that don't always work. And if they do, they may leave scars of shame or the lingering fear that if others knew about our malady, they would avoid or abandon us.

We may try an end run around God's grace. *God has more important things to concern himself with than our little old problems*, we tell ourselves. *We should be able to handle this*. We look at advertisements of people in excellent shape working out in gyms. We see before and after pictures of people who have lost weight by using the latest diet plan or supplement. We read self-help books by the score to improve our social lives or mental outlook without having to share ourselves with others. Attempts that keep us in isolation don't always go so well. I suspect God means for us to be in community. That way we can receive and also give help, even if all we do is offer understanding and share what worked for us. Many fine support programs have helped countless people overcome their difficulties, not in isolation, but in fellowship. If God wanted us to remain alone, God would only have created one of us.

PONDER

1. What do you think was going through the woman's mind as she made her way through the crowd toward Jesus?

2. What do you think was going through her mind when she realized she was healed?

3. Why do you think Jesus wanted to make this healing experience public?

4. Have you ever denied or minimized your need for God's help with a problem and tried to take care of it yourself? What happened?

5. What kind of environment makes it easier for people to acknowledge their challenges and vulnerabilities? How can you help create that type of environment for others?

PRAY

Jesus, grant me the humility to realize that there is nothing I need to hold back from your loving concern.

8

Jairus's Daughter

In God's Time, Not Ours

Then one of the leaders of the synagogue named Jairus came and, when he saw [Jesus], fell at his feet and begged him repeatedly, "My little daughter is at the point of death. Come and lay your hands on her, so that she may be made well, and live." So he went with him.

And a large crowd followed him and pressed in on him. Now there was a woman who had been suffering from hemorrhages for twelve years....She had heard about Jesus, and came up behind him in the crowd and touched his cloak, for she said, "If I but touch his clothes, I will be made well." Immediately her hemorrhage stopped...aware that power had gone forth from him, Jesus turned about in the crowd and said, "Who touched my clothes?"...He looked all around to see who had done it. But the woman, knowing what had happened to her, came in fear and trembling, fell down before him, and told him the whole truth. He said to her, "Daughter, your faith has made you well; go in peace, and be healed of your disease."

While he was still speaking, some people came from the leader's house to say, "Your daughter is dead.

Why trouble the teacher any further?" But overhearing what they said, "Jesus said to the leader of the synagogue, "Do not fear, only believe." He allowed no one to follow him except Peter, James, and John, the brother of James. When they came to the house of the leader of the synagogue, he saw a commotion, people weeping and wailing loudly. When he had entered, he said to them, "Why do you make a commotion and weep? The child is not dead but sleeping." And they laughed at him. Then he put them all outside and took the child's father and mother and those who were with him, and went in where the child was. He took her by the hand and said to her, "Talitha cum," which means, "Little girl, get up!" And immediately the girl got up and began to walk about (she was twelve years of age). At this they were overcome with amazement. He strictly ordered them that no one should know this, and told them to give her something to eat.

Mark 5:22–25; 27–30; 32–43

This chapter is about Jairus's daughter. Why interrupt it with the story of the hemorrhaging woman? If you're bothered by the interruption, how do you think Jairus felt? He was an established religious leader who had just tossed appearances to the wind by begging Jesus—a teacher of the fringe element—for help.

Jairus's daughter was "at the point of death." Time was of the essence. Jesus set off with him at once. How Jairus's hopes must have been raised. Each step brought healing closer to the dying child—until Jesus stopped dead in his tracks.

A woman who'd been suffering for twelve years—the entire lifetime of Jairus's daughter—reached out to touch Jesus' cloak. She didn't want to interrupt him or even be noticed. Once healed, she would have been happy to slip away. Jesus could easily have continued on his way without even breaking his stride; after all, the woman was already healed. For whatever reason, Jesus felt it was important enough to stop. He invited the woman to speak the truth so she could truly go in peace, healed not only of her bleeding problem but also of whatever else contributed to her distress.

I wonder what went through Jairus's mind. *My little girl is dying! Who cares who touched you? Please, Jesus, come on!* None of the Gospel accounts tell us that Jairus raised any objection. He must have been on tenterhooks. Maybe he was afraid to speak up, lest Jesus change his mind. Maybe he trusted Jesus enough to leave the matter in his hands. In any event, Jairus apparently waited in silence.

Meanwhile, messengers short on sensitivity arrived to tell Jairus, "Your daughter is dead. Why trouble the teacher any further?" I can only imagine what thoughts ran through Jairus's mind in that instant: *My baby is gone? My daughter is dead. Dead…and you're worried about me bothering Jesus? If Jesus hadn't stopped, maybe we'd have gotten home in time. I can't think. I can't breathe. I can't….*

But Jesus overheard the messengers. He told Jairus not to be afraid but to believe. Understandable as Jairus's sense of urgency was, and as much as we identify with it, Jesus didn't seem bothered by the timing. Jairus had demonstrated faith when he boldly broke protocol to implore Jesus' help. Jesus invited Jairus to continue trusting him, and protected that trust on the last leg of the journey. Detraction and derision erodes fragile faith. Jesus allowed no one to accompany them except the inner circle of faith-filled believers. When they arrived at Jairus's house, Jesus tried to quiet the commotion by reassuring people about the child. When they scoffed, Jesus put them out. With just a small circle of supportive followers and the child's parents,

Jesus took the little girl by the hand. He instructed her to get up and she did.

Jesus told the girl's parents to give her something to eat. Stunned by the miracle they'd just witnessed, maybe they didn't think about helping their daughter in such a practical way. Maybe they thought she was a ghost and didn't need food. Jesus made it quite clear that she was sound in mind and body and their family unit was restored.

SO MANY LESSONS

Jairus, moved by love, forgot about status and outward appearances. How often fear of what others think holds us back from acting in our own best interest or that of our loved ones. Is the approval of others really worth it?

Jairus placed his needs in Jesus' hands and he left them there, in spite of Jesus' delay. When we ask for God's help, change doesn't always happen on our timetable. Impatient, we often take back the reins and do something—anything—rather than endure the waiting, waiting, waiting. No doubt Jairus had strong feelings about Jesus stopping to help the other woman, but he waited on the sidelines nonetheless. What would have happened if Jairus had stalked home without waiting for Jesus? He may have reached his destination more quickly, but what would have been the point? He would have left the solution in the dust.

A spiritual director once told me, "Don't get ahead of God's grace." All our activity won't hurry God along. Some things just have to run their course. Sometimes, God has us wait while something is worked out in us, our loved ones, or in a third party. As writer Nikos Kazantzakis said, "God, it seems, is never in a hurry, while we are always in a hurry." It's okay. Nothing will slip past God. Even though Jesus was "still speaking" to the woman with the hemorrhage, he heard the messengers tell Jairus his daughter was dead.

When we trust God's healing power enough to turn to him in the first place, we're invited to continue to trust him over the long haul. As he was with Jairus, Jesus is with us and will continue to be with us on our healing journey. He will help us protect ourselves from demoralization. When we walk by faith and not by sight, we can tune out the voices that whisper—or even shout—messages of despair. Even though the messengers and mourners may have had Jairus's best interest at heart, their input was not helpful in that particular situation. We can nurture our sometimes-fragile faith by choosing a support network of fellow believers. If we seek, we will find. If we ask God to show us, God will lead us to the healthy, faith-filled support that we need in any given challenge.

Jesus not only told the girl to get up but also took her by the hand. God's part is to lead, guide, empower, and strengthen us. Our job is to respond and follow. When Jesus instructs us to get up out of our beds of doldrums, self-pity, or despair, we can respond by doing what we can. We don't have to be afraid. If we need help getting up, Jesus will provide that help. Like Jairus's daughter, our bodies need nourishment and attention. The Word became flesh and dwelt among us. Ever since the Son of God took on flesh and blood, we have living proof that spirit and matter are united. We can balance our nourishment of both if we want to enjoy health.

PONDER

Put yourself in Jairus's place:

1. As a religious official, how would you have felt throwing yourself down before Jesus and begging

for help? What makes it hard for you to ask for help?

2. As a parent, how would you have felt if the Master delayed dealing with your problem in order to help someone else? How do you deal with frustration when others don't attend to matters that you consider urgent?

3. As a beginner in trusting Jesus' power, how would you have felt when he invited you to disregard the voices of negativity? What helps you tune out negativity when your faith is wavering?

4. As witness to a miracle, how challenging would it have been for you to treat the daughter you'd received back from the dead in a normal, healthy way? How do you know when to let go and let God take over and when to provide others with what they need?

PRAY

Lord God, you always answer prayer, but the answers don't always come according to my expectations. Strengthen my fragile faith and help me tune out the voices of negativity.

9

A Silent Captive Healed

Speaking God's Truth in Love

[A] demoniac who was mute was brought to [Jesus]. And when the demon had been cast out, the one who had been mute spoke; and the crowds were amazed and said, "Never has anything like this been seen in Israel." But the Pharisees said, "By the ruler of the demons he casts out the demons."

Matthew 9:32–34

We aren't told anything about the mute who was healed. Maybe that's because no one knew much about him. How could they? Before his healing, the man probably communicated by making gestures or perhaps by writing. Anyone who's had laryngitis knows how laborious that can be, even today with widespread literacy, modern writing tools, and standardized sign language. It's especially challenging to share the shades of meaning of our thoughts and feelings. This man's inner life was trapped behind a wall of silence.

If the man had been mute since birth, what would his new ability to speak have been like? Would his speech have improved over time? When babies start talking, they begin with isolated words and gradually begin stringing them together to form complete ideas. On the other hand, we aren't told this particular mute was deaf. Perhaps having heard others speak and having an already developed adult brain, he was able to approximate speech patterns almost immediately.

No, we don't know anything about this man. What we do know is that once the demon was driven out, the man started speaking—perhaps for the first time in his life. I wonder what he said?

Maybe the man's first words were praise to God for his freedom from isolation. He may have felt a flood of gratitude for the simple joy of being able to share his inner life with the world around him! To ask for a drink of water, to express an opinion, or to ask or answer a question—each utterance was a triumph over silence. Maybe he thanked whoever had brought him to Jesus. That same person may have spent years anticipating the mute's needs and patiently deciphering his gestures.

Could the man's first words have been negative? What if he took the opportunity to express age-old grudges or complaints for hurts accumulated over a lifetime? What if he demanded things he'd always wanted but hadn't been able to ask for? What if he expressed self-pity for years of isolation? It's unlikely that he would have wasted his gift of speech on negativity. A heart and tongue bursting with gratitude seems a much more likely scenario.

DENYING GOODNESS

While the crowds were amazed by this demonstration of healing power, the Pharisees accused Jesus of being empowered by the prince of demons. Why? It probably had little to do with what the man said. The Pharisees' criticism might have been sour grapes. They may have envied Jesus' healing power and his resulting popularity—a popularity Jesus apparently tried to avoid by asking those healed to keep it to themselves. The

Pharisees may also have been driven by fear. Jesus' unorthodox teaching and ministry threatened the religious status quo. It also threatened the precarious relationship between the Jewish nation and Rome's occupying forces.

The Pharisees were correct in perceiving Jesus' challenge to the religious practices that had crystallized over the centuries. What they couldn't seem to grasp was that such change could be good and even holy. Those with the freedom to speak God's word had become boxed in by the details of observing the law. The Pharisees were probably pretty good at keeping the law—better than most, no doubt—but as Jesus pointed out elsewhere, their scrupulosity enabled them to strain out a gnat and swallow a camel (see Matt 23:24). Why else would these religious experts fail to see the inherent goodness of Jesus' actions? Jesus told his followers to judge a tree by its fruit (see Matt 7:15–20). His words were stronger when he warned the Pharisees that they would have to give an account of every useless word they spoke (see Matt 12:33–37).

WHEN IS SILENCE GOLDEN?

We aren't told how the demon prevented the man from speaking. Physical reasons aside, what holds us back from speaking what's in our hearts? Fear is one thing that springs to mind—fear of what others will think, fear of rejection, fear of consequences. Fear may not be a "demon" as we think of demons, but it certainly is not of God. The Bible is full of verses telling us not to be afraid. We're also told God is love and that perfect love casts out all fear (see 1 John 4:16; 18).

When we begin to face our fears, we still may need to learn how to share what's in our hearts with others. In order to develop that ability, it helps to listen to and then model others who communicate sincerely and effectively. Like a toddler learning to talk, we can learn a lot about speaking by first listening.

We who have the power of speech don't always use that ability wisely. Words can build up. They can also wound. There are times when we need to speak the truth even though it isn't easy. All of us have said things that, in retrospect, might have been better left unsaid. Many of us regret the harsh words spoken in anger. Critical and judgmental comments are seldom helpful. The mute had to wait a long time and had to be empowered by Christ before he spoke. When discussing sensitive issues, we would probably help ourselves and those around us if we paused to think things through before speaking. We can ask God to empower us to speak God's truth in love.

PONDER

1. After he was finally able to speak, what do you think the mute's first words were?
2. In what ways are you like the mute? What blocks you from speaking the truth?
3. How does connecting with Christ empower you to communicate more clearly with others?
4. When have the words you've spoken encouraged someone else? What was going on inside you prior to the conversation?
5. When have the words you've spoken been hurtful? What was going on inside you prior to that conversation? What might be some other ways to handle similar situations?

PRAY

Spirit of Truth, thank you for the gift of speech. May I use it to speak the truth in love.

10
_____

The Man with the Paralyzed Hand

Stretching Beyond Our Comfort Zone

Again [Jesus] entered the synagogue, and a man was there who had a withered hand. They watched him to see whether he would cure him on the sabbath, so that they might accuse him. And he said to the man who had the withered hand, "Come forward." Then he said to them, "Is it lawful to do good or to do harm on the sabbath, to save life or to kill?" But they were silent. He looked around at them with anger; he was grieved at their hardness of heart and said to the man, "Stretch out your hand." He stretched it out, and his hand was restored. The Pharisees went out and immediately conspired with the Herodians against him, how to destroy him.

Mark 3:1–6

Having one useless hand probably kept the man from doing many ordinary things. Perhaps it impacted his means of earning a livelihood. According to Luke's Gospel, the man's right and presumably dominant hand was impaired. Even so, the man probably had learned to make accommodations. Maybe he asked Jesus for healing. Maybe not. Nowhere in the Gospels does it say that the man called attention to himself or his condition. What all three Gospel accounts of this healing make clear is that the Pharisees were watching Jesus like a hawk. They wanted to see if he would break the law by healing the man on the Sabbath day of rest. They were looking for something they could hold against Jesus.

Luke's Gospel indicates that Jesus was well aware of what the religious authorities were thinking (Luke 6:8). If I had been in Jesus' position, I could easily see myself trying to avoid controversy, maybe even looking for a way to heal the man on the sly. Instead, Jesus called the man to the front of the synagogue where everyone could have a good view. Jesus not only healed the man in front of witnesses who were waiting with bated breath, but took the opportunity to address their unspoken question. Jesus put the crux of the issue right out in the open: Was the Sabbath a day for doing good or for being destructive? His opponents had an opportunity to voice their objection to Sabbath healing and explain their reasons, but they didn't take it. God's law had been twisted into a reason for failing to help others. Faced with this, the religious leaders remained silent. Were they intimidated? Was their position not as well thought out as it might have been? Were they ashamed or just speechless? In any event, for whatever reason, Jesus' opponents had no answer for him.

ONE CHALLENGE DECLINED, ANOTHER ACCEPTED

Still sensing their objection, Jesus was angered but also saddened. Their inflexible grip on the letter of the law prevented them from seeing the law's ultimate purpose: love of God, neighbor, and self. With no outward opposition forthcoming, Jesus told the man to stretch out his hand.

What was it like for that man at that moment of truth? By stretching out his hand, he would become an accomplice in

Sabbath-breaking. But if he failed to act at that time, he might never have had another opportunity to be healed. Sometimes it's now or never. As much as the man might have preferred to avoid controversy, he wanted something better than his status quo. He stretched out his hand. In following Jesus' direction, the man demonstrated his faith. From that moment on, the man could no longer be on the fence about Jesus. His action made a public declaration about which side of the controversy he was on. He would face whatever changes this declaration and his newly acquired wholeness would bring, but he could face them with two strong hands.

It was no surprise that those secure and comfortable in their social and religious standing were the most resistant to the spiritual renewal of Jesus' words and miracles. Upheaval of centuries of religious tradition would have left the keepers of that tradition very vulnerable. This would be true whether they were motivated by self-preservation or sincere concern for what they understood of God's will.

Although upholding a greater good, Jesus' action rejected legalistic compliance. No wonder the Pharisees wanted to find a way to kill him. For whatever reason, they weren't willing or able to challenge Jesus openly. Instead, they met in secret with members of Herod's party. Herod, the nominal king of the Jews, would also have been threatened by Jesus' challenge to the status quo. Behind-the-scenes conspiracy: what a contrast to Jesus' forthright demonstrations of bringing people to wholeness.

BRINGING IT CLOSER TO HOME

What happened to the man after he left the synagogue that day? Did he feel welcome to return on other Sabbaths? Did he stay in the town where he was known, or did he move on to another place to get a fresh start? Did he become one of Jesus' followers, always on the move? Was it challenging to deal with his newly acquired strength? What did he decide to do with it, and how did he make up his mind? We can only wonder.

More important, we can wonder what we would do with the strength we acquire when we accept Jesus' invitation to stretch out beyond our comfort zones. What would enable us to take a stand on some controversy we believe in or to face mindsets that have previously paralyzed us into inaction?

PONDER

1. Although the man with the withered hand had limitations prior to his healing, he was probably able to make do. What difficulties limit you? Are you are able to get by with them? How?
2. The man seized his opportunity for healing, even though it put him right in the middle of controversy. How do you know when reaching for some improvement is worth the risks?
3. The Pharisees said nothing when Jesus gave them the opportunity to express their objections openly. Why do you think they remained silent?
4. How does not dealing with an issue openly lead to deviousness?
5. What are some ways to counteract the challenges of confrontation?

PRAY

Jesus, grant me the willingness to cooperate with your healing action in my life today. Empower me to stretch beyond my comfort zone.

11

The Canaanite Woman's Daughter

The Pause That's Effective

Jesus left that place and went away to the district of Tyre and Sidon. Just then a Canaanite woman from that region came out and started shouting, "Have mercy on me, Lord, Son of David; my daughter is tormented by a demon." But he did not answer her at all. And his disciples came and urged him, saying, "Send her away, for she keeps shouting after us." He answered, "I was sent only to the lost sheep of the house of Israel." But she came and knelt before him, saying, "Lord, help me." He answered, "It is not fair to take the children's food and throw it to the dogs." She said, "Yes, Lord, yet even the dogs eat the crumbs that fall from their masters' table." Then Jesus answered her, "Woman, great is your faith! Let it be done for you as you wish." And her daughter was healed instantly.

Matthew 15:21–28

At first glance, Jesus' treatment of the woman sounds a bit harsh. In a closer look, we see that Jesus "went away" to the notoriously pagan territories of Tyre and Sidon, outside of Galilee. He couldn't have been too surprised that a Gentile approached him. After all, he was in Gentile territory.

We're told that Jesus didn't answer the woman, but we're not told why. Although it's easy to conclude that he was ignoring her, there are other possibilities. For all we know, he may have been formulating how to respond to her without seeming to neglect God's chosen people. Taking time before responding—especially under pressure—is effective. Remember the woman caught in adultery? When challenged to stone her and uphold the law, Jesus wrote in the dirt until he was ready to respond. The comment he made following that pause dispersed the angry crowd.

It was his disciples, not Jesus, who wanted him to send the woman away. Jesus' silence may have been to make it clear that his mission was first to the Jews, or to give the woman the opportunity to confirm the depth of her conviction.[1] That she did. She addressed Jesus not only as the Son of David, respecting his Jewish lineage, but also acknowledged him as her Lord. With her simple plea, she demonstrated her faith in Jesus and his power, her reverence for him, her love for someone other than herself, and her humility. She did not presume any merit or entitlement. She simply asked Jesus to have mercy on her. Her daughter's healing truly would have been an act of mercy for the woman herself. When those we love are suffering, what blesses them blesses us, too.

FOREIGN FAITH

Jesus first told the woman what she no doubt already knew; his mission was first to the people of Israel. Through the centuries, these chosen people had been the caretakers of God's promise to send a savior. Jesus said that it wasn't fair to take food from the children and give it to the dogs. That statement wasn't quite as harsh as it sounds. In this Gospel passage, the Greek word used for dogs, *kunarios*, is closer in meaning to the word "puppies," young dogs still dependent on a parent for their needs.[2]

The woman didn't argue. Instead, her response implied two things about God's grace: (1) it had already been given to the people of Israel and rightly so, and (2) it was so abundant that there was plenty left over for others, too. This was not new thinking. The Old Testament prophesied that the Messiah would be a light to the Gentiles. The story of the Magi, foreigners who worshipped Jesus, marked the manifestation (epiphany) that Jesus was the Savior not only of Israel but also of all nations.

Earlier in Matthew's Gospel, Jesus himself told the Jews that if the miracles he had performed in their presence "had been done in Tyre and Sidon, they would have repented long ago" and that on the Judgment Day, things would go better "for Tyre and Sidon" than for his Jewish audience (Matt 11:21–22). Maybe it was no coincidence that Jesus left Israelite territory and headed for Tyre and Sidon.

This Canaanite woman was living proof of Jesus' words. She wasn't privy to the chosen people's heritage, and yet she took the leap of faith. She made her need and sorrow known to Jesus and entrusted herself and her daughter completely to God's love and mercy. The fact that her request was not answered immediately did not deter her. Her persistence simply demonstrated the strength of her faith until Jesus affirmed that her daughter would be healed. This foreigner was a living example that the people of Tyre and Sidon had greater faith with less evidence than the chosen ones.

IN HER SHOES

It's easy to understand the Canaanite woman's position. She responded with an ironic combination of bold persistence and sincere humility. Often, when our loved ones are suffering, we would willingly suffer in their place if we could. Our anguish matches their pain. As caregivers, we willingly endure sleepless nights, bedside vigils, or weary trips to and from the hospital. We do everything in our power to alleviate their discomfort. Empathy and loving concern can make us brave, too. Long after we have worn out our welcome, we persist in seeking answers, remedies, or alternatives from health care providers. We risk being "the squeaky wheel" to intercede for our loved ones.

Sometimes we're like helpless puppies, scrambling around in a knot of directionless love and energy. We need the guidance and support of someone not so vulnerable to excitability. In addition to seeking healing on a practical, medical level, and the help and comfort of those around us, let's remember that the Divine Healer is always available. It's challenging when our prayers for healing don't result in the hoped-for outcome, or when God seems not to answer our prayers at all. Even so, let's not stop trusting that God is in charge and that God loves our loved ones even more than we do. When we've done all that we can, it's okay to leave the rest in God's hands. It's also okay to cry out to God in pain, frustration, anger, or fear, as long as we keep talking to God. Feelings come and feelings go. We can share them sincerely with God and know that God is always there, always listening, even when we seem to get no answers. God always has something in mind.

PONDER

1. "Have mercy on me, Lord, Son of David; my daughter is tormented by a demon." With her simple plea, the Canaanite woman revealed her faith in Jesus, her recognition of Jesus' power, her acknowledgment of Jesus as her personal Lord, her

humility, and her love for her suffering daughter. Why are these elements important in prayer? In what ways are these elements present in your prayers of supplication? Can you name any other important elements of prayer?

2. Jesus did not answer the woman's appeal immediately. Under what circumstances is it helpful to remain silent before responding to another person?

3. What are some ways to continue trusting God when it seems like your prayers are not being answered?

PRAY

God, when my loved ones are hurting, help me remember that you love them even more than I do.

NOTES

1. Catholic Bible commentary compiled in 1859 by the late Rev. George Leo Haydock, following the Douay-Rheims Bible, http://haydock1859.tripod.com/id33.html.

2. Ibid.

12

The Boy with an Evil Spirit

How Much Faith Is Enough?

When [Jesus, Peter, James, and John] came to the disciples, they saw a great crowd around them, and some scribes arguing with them. When the whole crowd saw [Jesus], they were immediately overcome with awe, and they ran forward to greet him. He asked them, "What are you arguing about with them?" Someone from the crowd answered him, "Teacher, I brought you my son; he has a spirit that makes him unable to speak; and whenever it seizes him, it dashes him down; and he foams and grinds his teeth and becomes rigid; and I asked your disciples to cast it out, but they could not do so." He answered them, "You faithless generation, how much longer must I be among you? How much longer must I put up with you? Bring him to me." And they brought the boy to him. When the spirit saw him, immediately it convulsed the boy, and he fell on the ground and rolled about, foaming at the mouth. Jesus asked the father, "How long has this been happening to him?" And he said, "From childhood. It has often cast him into the fire and into the water, to destroy him; but if you are able to do anything, have pity on us and help us."

> Jesus said to him, "If you are able!—All things can be
> done for the one who believes." Immediately the
> father of the child cried out, "I believe; help my unbe-
> lief!" When Jesus saw that a crowd came running
> together, he rebuked the unclean spirit, saying to it,
> "You spirit that keeps this boy from speaking and
> hearing, I command you, come out of him, and never
> enter him again!" After crying out and convulsing
> him terribly, it came out, and the boy was like a
> corpse, so that most of them said, "He is dead." But
> Jesus took him by the hand and lifted him up, and he
> was able to stand. When he had entered the house,
> his disciples asked him privately, "Why could we not
> cast it out?" He said to them, "This kind can come out
> only through prayer."
>
> Mark 9:14–29

Jesus was returning from the mountain where he'd been gloriously
transfigured in front of Peter, James, and John. In Jesus' absence,
the other disciples apparently had been left to contend with those
who were seeking Jesus. When he returned, they were embroiled
in a dispute with the religious scribes. A nameless man had asked
those remaining disciples to cure his son, but they were unable to
do so. It's unclear exactly why, although Jesus later told them that
such situations could only be dealt with by prayer.

In their defense, those disciples had not had the moun-
taintop experience that Peter, James, and John had. Perhaps feelings of self-doubt, envy, or self-pity at being left behind interfered
with their ability to pray. When we doubt our abilities, it's difficult to move beyond our absorption in our own inadequacies
and reach out to others. On the other hand, perhaps the crowd
lacked confidence in the second string team's ability to teach and
heal. The father related his son's affliction and the disciples' inef-

fectiveness to Jesus. In response, Jesus seemed to ask how long he would have to put up with people who lacked faith. Was his frustration with the crowd, his disciples, or both?

Nevertheless, Jesus' frustration didn't override his mercy. He had the boy brought to him. Whatever negative force was at work inside the boy had a fit when it encountered Jesus. That probably didn't promote confidence in Jesus. The father followed up by saying, "If you are able to do anything, have pity on us and help us." Well aware that his son's condition was long-standing, the man's "if" implies a world of doubt. In contrast, many people who sought healing from Jesus simply cried out, "Lord, have mercy." They didn't doubt Jesus' power but asked only that he take pity on them and use that power.

FAITH REVEALED IN TRUTH

Yet, in spite of his shaky confidence, this desperate father reached out. Jesus addressed this weak link, saying, "If you [yourself] are able!—All things can be done for the one who believes." Things are done for the believer; he's the recipient, not the agent. Nevertheless, the recipient's contribution of belief is essential. Sensing this, the father mustered all the faith he could while acknowledging the truth: it was inadequate. "I believe; help my unbelief." Although knowing it was not enough, he gave Jesus all he had. Jesus transformed this father's admission of limited faith into sufficiency just as he had fed a multitude with the ridiculously insufficient five loaves and two fish.

SOMETIMES THINGS GET WORSE BEFORE THEY GET BETTER

Jesus expelled the destructive spirit from the boy, but it struck one final blow, leaving the boy for dead. Destructive tendencies wreak havoc in our lives, tossing us from one problem to another. We endure or watch our loved ones endure calamities such as physical illness, emotional pain, or life crises. Often we're powerless to stop the downward spiral. Sometimes it just isn't possible to move in a healthier direction until we hit bottom and there's nowhere to go but up. If it feels like we're dying, there's good reason. We die to an old way of life. When that happens, there doesn't seem to be any way to rise to new life unless God lifts us up.

When faced with a long-standing problem or illness, many of us barely dare to hope. Like the boy's father, we can't seem to mobilize even a mustard seed of faith. But maybe we don't need to. What if all we have is a fraction of a mustard seed of faith? If we have just enough faith to approach God and speak the truth about our lack of trust, then that, in itself, is an act of faith. Trusting God enough to admit the truth about our vulnerability is a vote of confidence, not in us, but in him. Isn't that faith? Didn't Jesus tell us that those who know they are spiritually poor are blessed?

PONDER

1. When the nine disciples couldn't heal the man's son, apparently they were drawn into an argument, or at least a debate, with the religious experts. Why might lack of effectiveness invite arguments?

2. The spirit made the boy unable to speak. It also threw him around against his will and made him grind his teeth. When has being unable to express what is going on inside of you been like being tossed around against your will? When has lack of communication ever caused you to grit your teeth?

3. When have you felt like crying out to God, "I believe; help my unbelief!"? Under what circumstances might that declaration strengthen faith?
4. The boy received one final blow from the evil spirit before he was completely healed. How does that inspire you to persevere?

PRAY

Lord of life, grant me the courage to endure the healing process as my old, unhealthy behaviors die. Raise me up to new life in you.

13

Jesus Blesses Little Children

Healing Self-Esteem

People were bringing little children to [Jesus] in order
that he might touch them; and the disciples spoke
sternly to them. But when Jesus saw this, he was
indignant and said to them, "Let the little children
come to me; do not stop them; for it is to such as these
that the kingdom of God belongs. Truly I tell you,
whoever does not receive the kingdom of God as a little child will never enter it." And he took them up in
his arms, laid his hands on them, and blessed them.

Mark 10:13–16

People crowded in on Jesus wherever he went. It's understandable that his followers tried to whittle the crowds to manageable
size. It's even understandable that they would screen out little
children. The disciples probably didn't think blessing children
was all that important in light of Jesus' mission. What could little children understand of his wisdom? Many people who sought
Jesus were suffering from severe disabilities. Compared to them,
parents who wanted a blessing for their children must have
seemed a low priority, if not inconsequential. Why wouldn't the
disciples screen them out?

But Jesus had a way of noticing the disenfranchised, the overlooked, the outright rejects of society. Jesus saw the inherent preciousness of each of his Father's beloved. That included everyone: old and young, rich and poor, respectable and shameful. Our worth comes from the fact that we are all children of God, regardless of what we have accomplished or failed to accomplish, who we know or don't know, or whether or not we have the intellectual capacity to analyze Jesus' teaching in light of Scripture study.

Jesus scolded his disciples for discriminating against the children. In doing so, he conferred on the little ones a value that only he and their parents had recognized. He loved them for who they were at that moment, before they had the opportunity to make very many life choices. Perhaps his blessing would impact every choice those children made in their lives from that point on. What the children could absorb—whether they could explain it or not—is that they were welcomed by Jesus and treated with kindness. The Gospel said that he took them up in his arms before laying hands on them and blessing them. Think of that image: he lifted each one up and held them in his loving embrace, if only for a moment, and then blessed them before handing them back to their parents' care. What more powerful sermon could there be about their worth as children of God and the nature of that God?

THE CHALLENGE OF RESPECT

Children respond so well to respect. Don't we all? When thinking of the people who have made a difference in our lives, the most knowledgeable or powerful don't always come to mind. The people who impacted our lives and helped us tap into our potential are often the ones who made us feel like we were important to them. Knowing someone takes an interest in us personally can make us want to be better people. In order to grow and thrive, we not only need examples or instruction but validation that who we are is okay. That builds the self-esteem that gives us courage to pursue our goals in spite of setbacks. We can risk challenges because we know that our self-worth won't be annihilated even if we fail sometimes. Much as we find that to be true in our own lives, it's not always easy to remember it in our interactions with others.

Depending on what we're contending with on any given day, the concerns of those around us can seem trivial. Sometimes, that may be true whether we're dealing with children or with other adults. But even though we can't—and shouldn't—give in to incessant or unrealistic demands, we can say no to those requests with respect. We can listen to others as if they were worth our time, even if the time we have to give is not as much as they (or we) would like. We can correct others without crushing their spirits by criticizing the behavior, not the person—a tall order! We might not always have the patience or emotional wherewithal to act the way we'd like. That's okay. We can treat ourselves the same way, knowing that who we are is okay even though we sometimes lose our tempers, misplace our attention, or fall short in some other way.

Time alone with Jesus can remind us that we are loved and valued in spite of our shortcomings. We can allow ourselves to be lifted up by his loving embrace. We can also allow ourselves to be blessed with the awareness that others—even those we (or society) might not regard very highly—are worthy of our respect. When we forget, we can forgive ourselves and move on. Jesus didn't say his disciples were worthless for rejecting the children. He didn't say they couldn't be his disciples anymore for that or for any of their other failings. He called them on their behavior, let them know why it was wrong, and told them what to do instead. He calls us to be like little children in order to belong to the kingdom of God. What if we allowed ourselves to be lifted up by Jesus, if only for a moment, each day? We could then face each day blessed with the ability to go forward treating others with respect that comes from knowing we ourselves are worthy of respect.

PONDER

1. The disciples thought they were helping Jesus by filtering out the children. When have you done something you thought was helpful only to discover you were part of the problem? How were you made aware of the fact that your behavior wasn't helpful? What happened?
2. When do you feel most like a little child? Do you feel closer to Jesus at those times? Why or why not?
3. Why do you suppose people cannot receive the kingdom of God unless they receive it as a little child?
4. When do you find it most challenging to treat others with the respect you yourself would like? What are some ways to move beyond those challenges?

PRAY

Jesus, you took the little children in your arms. When I feel small and helpless, may I rest quietly in your loving embrace.

14

The Rich Man

A Custom-Made Antidote

As [Jesus] was setting out on a journey, a man ran up and knelt before him, and asked him, "Good Teacher, what must I do to inherit eternal life?" Jesus said to him, "Why do you call me good? No one is good but God alone. You know the commandments: 'You shall not murder; You shall not commit adultery; You shall not steal; You shall not bear false witness; You shall not defraud; Honor your father and mother.'" He said to him, "Teacher, I have kept all these since my youth." Jesus, looking at him, loved him and said, "You lack one thing; go, sell what you own, and give the money to the poor, and you will have treasure in heaven; then come, follow me." When he heard this, he was shocked and went away grieving, for he had many possessions.

Mark 10:17–22

The man asked what he had to do to inherit eternal life. He didn't say *gain* or *earn*, but *inherit*—that is, receive eternal life. When Jesus reminded the man of the commandments, the man said he had kept them since he was young. The man's own heart seemed to tell him there was more to eternal life than complying with the Law.

Jesus then looked at the man with love. Perhaps he saw potential in the man's heartfelt desire for something more. Jesus offered him that opportunity and invited the man to join him. Jesus didn't invite everyone he encountered to follow him. Many he told to go on their way or sent them back to their homes. Jesus invited this man to follow him, but the man didn't accept the invitation. Instead, he went away sad.

Why? Maybe the key is in the commandment Jesus didn't mention: Thou shalt not covet (see Exod 20:17). The man was rich. Whether he got his wealth honestly or not didn't seem to matter. He was inordinately attached to his possessions. The *Oxford American Dictionary* says the word *covet* means to "desire eagerly." This man's desire for wealth had been attained but not quenched. He coveted his riches and the lifestyle they guaranteed. As genuine as his desire for eternal life seemed to be, when the man probed a bit deeper, Jesus loved him enough to answer honestly. The only thing the man lacked was the ability to give up his possessions.

We can't inherit eternal life unless we're open to receive it. To receive a gift, we have to open our hands in order to accept it from the giver. We can't embrace God's gift of eternal life if our arms are tightly wrapped around some other source of security.

INDIVIDUAL DIFFERENCES

Jesus wasn't opposed to wealth. He didn't tell Zacchaeus he was required to give up all his wealth (see Luke 19:1–10). St. Paul didn't say money is the root of all evil. He said, "the *love* of money is a root of all kinds of evil" (1 Tim 6:10, emphasis mine). Wealth isn't evil in itself, but the obsessive desire and focus on wealth blocks us from following God's call to love. When we depend solely on our own resources, we can't receive the kingdom with complete reliance on God. It's okay to be prudent about our finances in order to pay our way and live reasonably securely. But when we make an idol out of our finances, that's when our riches become problematic for our spiritual growth.

Not everyone is called to give up in the same way because not everyone covets in the same way. Some of us treasure our reputations, our good name, or our status. Some of us treasure physical pleasure. Some of us may covet the approval of friends and family. Enjoying these things is not bad in itself, but when we covet or become dependent on them, we're drawn away from God's kingdom of love. When we crave approval, we may go along with the crowd rather than follow our own conscience. When we crave pleasure or relief from pain to an extreme, we may find ourselves addicted to one or another substance or behavior. Coveting a good reputation may lead us away from honesty as we attempt to cover up truths that reflect on us unfavorably.

Any number of things can block us from receiving the kingdom of God. The one thing that we rely on the most may be the very thing that Jesus, in his love for us, invites us to leave behind. We may not be bad or evil if we don't relinquish that which we cling to, but it will certainly block our spiritual growth. The hardest thing to let go of will always be whatever we believe is the source of our security, pleasure, or identity. *Anything but that*, we think. It is just that very thing, however, that holds us back from abandoning ourselves completely to the care of God.

We can understand why the rich man was shocked by Jesus' proposition. Perhaps he had been confident that, since he felt he had kept the commandments so well, it wouldn't be all that challenging to progress to the next step. Had he purposely avoided looking at the one commandment that was beyond his reach? Or was he in denial?

The rich man went away, very sad, because he wasn't able to choose following Jesus over his own riches. As Jesus said, "For where your treasure is, there your heart will be also" (Matt 6:21). As we think about the things we treasure, we can be reassured that Jesus is looking at us with love. God wants our hearts. The choice is ours.

PONDER

1. The rich man seemed confident that he had kept the commandments since he was young. Why do you suppose that he asked Jesus what more he had to do to inherit eternal life?
2. When have you felt called by Jesus to do more than you were capable of? What happened?
3. One of the Ten Commandments tells us not to covet. How can you avoid coveting when you have natural needs and wants?
4. What's the difference between receiving eternal life and achieving it?
5. In what ways would eternal life be different from the life you have today?

PRAY

Loving Savior, like the rich man, show me what I need to let go of to continue my spiritual journey. Help me trust that what I gain will be much better than what I surrender.

15
_____

A Deaf Man Cured

Being Opened to God

Then [Jesus] returned from the region of Tyre, and
went by way of Sidon towards the Sea of Galilee, in the
region of the Decapolis. They brought to him a deaf
man who had an impediment in his speech; and they
begged him to lay his hand on him. He took him aside
in private, away from the crowd, and put his fingers
into his ears, and he spat and touched his tongue. Then
looking up to heaven, he sighed and said to him,
"Ephphatha," that is, "Be opened." And immediately
his ears were opened, his tongue was released, and he
spoke plainly. Then Jesus ordered them to tell no one;
but the more he ordered them, the more zealously they
proclaimed it. They were astounded beyond measure,
saying, "He has done everything well; he even makes
the deaf to hear and the mute to speak."

Mark 7:31–37

Who brought the deaf man to Jesus? Whoever "they" were, they
obviously loved the man enough to want him healed. Why did
Jesus feel the need to take the man away from them and heal him
in private? Did Jesus just want to prevent people from witnessing

the miracle? He often urged people to keep quiet about the miraculous healings, but they never did. On the other hand, Jesus often healed people in front of crowds, sometimes boldly healing them on the Sabbath in plain sight. Why did Jesus heal this deaf man in private? We may never know while we're on this side of heaven.

Maybe, as when he healed Jairus's daughter privately, Jesus wanted to avoid doubters who might have discouraged the man's faith. But what about those people who brought the man to Jesus? Maybe the man had to be separated from his loved ones— at least for a time—in order for the healing to be effective. Well-meaning loved ones can't always be part of our healing process. Sometimes they simply don't have the resources. Sometimes they have issues that prevent them from cooperating with what is needed for our healing. When the healing process is foreign to them or beyond their comprehension, they may not even be able to encourage us from the sidelines.

The deaf man's family loved him enough to bring him to Jesus. They may have grieved that he could never hear them or share his own thoughts clearly. Over the years, a pattern may have evolved whereby he relied on his family, and they became used to being his link to the world. Welcome as his recovery might seem, what if the thought of his independence threatened his family? What if the loss of his family as intermediaries was threatening to the man himself? Maybe he needed to rely directly and exclusively on Jesus. It is said that God has no grandchildren. To have a mature faith of our own, sooner or later, we need to develop our own connection with God, independent of the faith legacy we received from our parents.

Once they were alone, Jesus put his fingers into the man's ears, then spat and touched the man's tongue. In that culture, saliva was believed to have healing properties. Jesus' use of an accepted manner of healing probably reassured the man. Jesus then looked up to heaven and sighed. (According to the Good

News Translation, Jesus gave a deep groan.) Whether Jesus sighed or groaned, it would seem that this healing tapped into something deep within Jesus. It's as if this particular healing required Jesus to connect with his heavenly Father in a clear, outward way. Only then, does Jesus say, "Be opened." Once he did, his direction to "be opened" took effect.

OPENING THE LINES OF COMMUNICATION

After Jesus' touch, the man's ears were able to make sense of what others—including his own family—were trying to communicate. The Gospel passage indicates that the man may have been able to speak prior to the healing but had an impediment. Once his tongue was touched by Jesus and his ears were opened, the man was able to speak clearly. It's amazing how much the ability to speak clearly involves the ability to hear what others are saying. How else can we have any common ground for communicating effectively?

Sometimes the ones we love the most are the ones we have the most trouble communicating with. Over years, unhealthy patterns of selective listening or negativity can lead to misunderstanding. We may hear our loved ones without really listening. Distractions, lack of interest, or subjects that hit too close to home can make tuning people out easy or even inviting. Conversely, we may feel like we're wasting our breath when others seem unable or unwilling to hear us or validate the feelings we're trying to express. We beat around the bush when it feels too risky to share what is in our hearts. We don't want to upset the apple cart. Fear can impair our ability to speak honestly or listen when others speak their hearts.

Maybe Jesus separated the deaf-mute from his loved ones until the man could become grounded in his own identity as a child of God. Perhaps then the man could afford to hear what his family had to say and had the courage to speak his mind with honesty and kindness. After all, a little bit of Christ had mingled with his own tongue.

When we find it challenging to speak our own hearts and minds, or when we notice ourselves turning a deaf ear to the needs of others, maybe we need to take some time to be alone with God. Before his healing, the man was silent in Jesus' presence. Can we dare to be silent in Jesus' presence until he opens our ears to hear what he wants us to hear and speak the words he would like us to say to others?

PONDER

1. Those who loved the deaf-mute brought him to Jesus to be healed. How do you think they felt when Jesus took their loved one away from them in order to heal him?
2. Have you ever been separated from a loved one during their healing process or your own? What happened? Why might it be necessary for loved ones to be apart in order for healing to occur?
3. How is being able to hear what others have to say related to being able to speak effectively?
4. What in you needs to "be opened"? How can spending time with God in silence help?

PRAY

Holy Spirit, when I find myself deaf to others or unable to speak my mind and heart, open the lines of communication blocked by ego or fear.

16

The Blind Man at Bethsaida

Clearing Our Field of Vision

> They came to Bethsaida. Some people brought a blind
> man to [Jesus] and begged him to touch him. He took
> the blind man by the hand and led him out of the vil-
> lage; and when he had put saliva on his eyes and laid
> his hands on him, he asked him, "Can you see any-
> thing?" And the man looked up and said, "I can see
> people, but they look like trees, walking." Then Jesus
> laid his hands on his eyes again; and he looked
> intently and his sight was restored, and he saw every-
> thing clearly. Then [Jesus] sent him away to his home,
> saying, "Do not even go into the village."
>
> Mark 8:22–26

The people begged Jesus to touch the blind man. Jesus did so
much more. Those who brought the man to Jesus probably led
him by the hand. Jesus took him by the hand and led him out of
the village. At that point, he no longer had his loved ones to lead
him. He had to depend solely on Jesus. What did that feel like?
Was the blind man relieved that he had been handed over to the
care of someone who had healing power? Or was he scared to
have only a stranger as his guide? Either way, he had little choice.

To stay with his familiar support group meant reconciling himself to the status quo.

I've heard that if a drowning man is panicky, the lifeguard sometimes has to render him even more helpless in order to save him. Only when the victim has no alternative but to rely on the lifeguard can he be saved. Perhaps that's why Jesus had to get the man off by himself—to ensure complete dependence on Jesus alone with no option but to surrender. Jesus put saliva on the man's eyes and laid hands on him. This probably reassured the man because saliva was a commonly accepted treatment in that culture.

ONCE IS NOT ENOUGH

After laying his hands on the man, Jesus asked him if he could see anything. Jesus didn't usually ask the people he healed if the healing had taken effect. He commanded and it was done. "Be opened" and the deaf-mute heard and spoke. "Pick up your mat and go home" and the lame man walked. This man was different. "Can you see anything?" Jesus asked. Chances are, Jesus didn't doubt his own power. Although some healing did occur, perhaps Jesus sensed something blocking this man's receptivity. The man said he saw people, but that they looked like trees walking around. Perhaps he had been blind since birth. In that case, how would he know what he was seeing? Maybe that was the problem. Having never seen people before, he may have had a different expectation of what they'd look like. Maybe reality didn't fit in with his preconception.

In any event, Jesus was not content to leave a job half-done. He laid his hands on the man's eyes again. This time the man "looked intently" and could finally see clearly. Jesus wasn't satisfied leaving the man with partially restored sight. Accepting faulty vision as being accurate might have been worse than not being able to see at all. It might have left the man thinking his distorted perception was reality, which would have been a more insidious blindness.

Once the man saw clearly, Jesus advised him to go to his home without even going to the village. Did Jesus simply want to avoid the hoopla that always followed his miracles? Or did he know it would take time for the man to make sense of the barrage of new images? Maybe time to process his new vision in solitude was part of his healing.

CLEARING OUR FIELD OF VISION

Sometimes we lose our bearings. We feel lost. We may be torn among possible alternatives. At certain turning points, decisions need to be made, and no one can make those decisions for us. We may long to be led by the hand, but whose hand should we grasp? Those may be the times that Jesus needs to get us off on our own, in order to help us see clearly. He may have to remove the things that usually capture our attention: busy schedules, familiar routines, or even family and friends. Geographic distance, circumstances, or a crisis of faith at 2 a.m. can cut us off from our usual connections. Ironically, it might be the solitude resulting from an illness that brings the opportunity for new growth. We may feel more vulnerable when it's just God and us. Nevertheless, we can be reassured. Just as Jesus led the blind man by the hand, we can trust that he is guiding us to clarity. That clarity might come gradually, as it did for the blind man. We may get inklings of the truth but not be ready to face the whole truth all at once. God knows what we can handle.

Perhaps our vision is limited by self-centeredness. We sometimes view the people in our lives as if they were walking scenery, not individuals with their own needs and wants. They're there to lean on when we're tired of standing on our own, or if we want the benefits of their growth and efforts. God isn't satisfied with that. Once we're able to see that we are taking people for granted, God will help us develop our vision further. If we are willing to "look intently" at those around us, it will be possible to see them in their humanity. When we consider their needs and triumphs, their joys and sorrows, we'll see they are just like us. Our vision will enable us to relate more completely to the world around us.

Like the man healed of his blindness, we may need some time to digest this truth about ourselves and process how best to relate to the people that make up our community.

PONDER

1. How do you think the blind man felt as he was handed over from those who loved him to Jesus' care?
2. Can spending time alone with God in meditation be reassuring and intimidating at the same time? In what ways?
3. When are you most likely to view the people around you as living scenery? When are you most likely to consider others as individuals with the same feelings, pressures, and weaknesses as you?
4. How can you practice looking more intently at the world around you? What might you see if you do?

PRAY

Loving God, sometimes I regard the people in my life as nothing more than walking scenery. Help me look intently at others and see them clearly as your beloved children.

17

Blind Bartimaeus

Seizing Opportunity

They came to Jericho. As [Jesus] and his disciples and a large crowd were leaving Jericho, Bartimaeus son of Timaeus, a blind beggar, was sitting by the roadside. When he heard that it was Jesus of Nazareth, he began to shout out and say, "Jesus, Son of David, have mercy on me!" Many sternly ordered him to be quiet, but he cried out even more loudly, "Son of David, have mercy on me!" Jesus stood still and said, "Call him here." And they called the blind man, saying to him, "Take heart; get up, he is calling you." So throwing off his cloak, he sprang up and came to Jesus. Then Jesus said to him, "What do you want me to do for you?" The blind man said to him, "My teacher, let me see again." Jesus said to him, "Go; your faith has made you well." Immediately he regained his sight and followed [Jesus] on the way.

Mark 10:46–52

Unlike those who sought Jesus or were brought to him by others, Bartimaeus just happened to be sitting by the side of the road. A busy roadside was probably a good place to beg. When Bartimaeus heard that Jesus was within earshot, he began crying out for mercy.

People in the crowd tried to shut him up. For years, Bartimaeus probably sat in the same spot, humbly asking for alms. Were people annoyed at his sudden assertiveness? Did they dismiss the blind beggar as not worth Jesus' trouble? Maybe they feared that if Bartimaeus got Jesus' attention, their own requests might go unmet. It was the people in front who ordered Bartimaeus to be quiet (see Luke 18:39). Who knows why people are uncharitable or discourage others from getting help?

PEER PRESSURE

Their scolding didn't stop Bartimaeus. He tried even harder. It's as if the crowd's response heightened his awareness that he was on his own. Direct contact with the Son of David was his only hope for healing. Opportunity had come within his limited grasp, and he didn't intend to miss it. So he didn't knuckle under to peer pressure. He not only persisted, but he cried out all the more. Sure enough, Jesus heard his cry and stopped. Taking time from his own journey to attend to the needs of another, Jesus called the blind man to him.

Once Bartimaeus had Jesus' attention, the crowd jumped on the bandwagon to encourage him. Maybe they were afraid that Jesus wouldn't help them if they didn't show interest in someone Jesus cared about. Or maybe witnessing the kindness of one human being to another made them want to do likewise.

DOING WHAT HE COULD

When he heard Jesus' call, Bartimaeus threw off his coat. It's possible the sudden flush of excitement overheated him. More likely, he didn't want any encumbrance to trip him up or slow him down. When he arrived at Jesus' feet, what he needed was clearly evident. Still, Jesus asked him, "What do you want me to do for you?" What we need and what we want isn't always the same thing. Bartimaeus asked to see *again*. Apparently, Bartimaeus at one time may have had the power of sight and somehow lost it. Jesus told him to go, saying his faith had made him well. His faith and Jesus' word restored his sight. Once he could see clearly, what did he do? He followed Jesus.

Bartimaeus's limited ability had prevented him from pursuing healing in a proactive way. It didn't matter. He didn't need to do more than he was capable of; he just needed to do what he could. We may be homebound by illness or family responsibilities, or limited in our activity by any number of things. That's okay. God is always within our reach and will always meet us where we are. It is said that God will do for us what we can't do for ourselves. On the other hand, we do need to do what we can do for ourselves. What we can do may include resisting the urge to go along with the crowd. Some of us don't want to make waves or stick out like the proverbial sore thumb. We'd rather blend into the background. But when the opportunity to live more fully presents itself, we can become all that God has in mind for us to be. We don't have to let the reaction of others or their lack of encouragement stop us.

By the same token, how do we react when someone in our family or social group wants to reach out for something better? Are we supportive or do we feel threatened? Do we jealously guard our own opportunities, thinking someone else's success somehow makes less success available for us? What keeps us from genuinely encouraging others to "go for it"?

JESUS' CALL TO US

When Bartimaeus heard Jesus' call, he threw off his cloak. It's easy to wrap ourselves in comfortable trappings. But sometimes those things we cling to for comfort are the very things that keep us from getting to the core of our problems. Our security blankets can mask the issues that need addressing or lull us into a faulty sense of well-being.

Physical comforts are nice, but they don't always satisfy the needs we have for a deeper relationship with God, with other people, and with our own selves. Tasty treats are enjoyable, but no quantity of food or alcohol will satisfy our deeper hunger. We all need time to relax. Recreation is good and necessary, but hours of mindless entertainment and superficial relationships can keep us from seeing matters that God is calling us to address for our own well-being and that of others.

Bartimaeus threw down his cloak. It wasn't pried away from him. He seemed happy to let it go. Why? Because he had the hope of something better. Nobody willingly lets go of crutches such as denial if the only prospect is a painful status quo. But like Bartimaeus, we have the hope of something better—an encounter with God that will restore our clarity and equip us to handle reality at any given moment. Like Bartimaeus, once we see clearly, we may decide that our best course will be to continue to follow where God is leading.

PONDER

1. In his blindness, Bartimaeus wasn't free to seek out Jesus. Nevertheless, Jesus came within his reach. When have you seen someone touched by God even though they were unable to reach out on their own?

2. When Bartimaeus cried out for mercy, those around him told him to be quiet. Who is crying out for mercy in the world, in your community, in your family? Are they being silenced or encouraged? Why?

3. What do you think enabled Bartimaeus to keep crying out in spite of peer pressure to be quiet?
4. When Jesus called him, Bartimaeus threw down his cloak. What encumbrances might keep you from answering Jesus' call to you?

PRAY

Risen Christ, fill me with hope. Enable me to discard any security blanket—no matter how comfortable—that hinders my response to your call.

18

The Crippled Woman

Freed from What Weighs Us Down

Now [Jesus] was teaching in one of the synagogues on the sabbath. And just then there appeared a woman with a spirit that had crippled her for eighteen years. She was bent over and was quite unable to stand up straight. When Jesus saw her, he called her over and said, "Woman, you are set free from your ailment." When he laid his hands on her, immediately she stood up straight and began praising God. But the leader of the synagogue, indignant because Jesus had cured on the sabbath, kept saying to the crowd, "There are six days on which work ought to be done; come on those days and be cured, and not on the sabbath day." But the Lord answered him and said, "You hypocrites! Does not each of you on the sabbath untie his ox or his donkey from the manger, and lead it away to give it water? And ought not this woman, a daughter of Abraham whom Satan bound for eighteen long years, be set free from this bondage on the sabbath day?" When he said this, all his opponents were put to shame; and the entire crowd was rejoicing at all the wonderful things that he was doing.

Luke 13:10–17

The crippled woman didn't ask for healing. Jesus noticed her, saw her plight, and took the initiative. It's possible that the woman's appearance in the synagogue signaled her desire for healing. The synagogue leader told the crowd to come for healing on other days, rather than on the Sabbath. Presumably, many of the people crowding the synagogue that day were there seeking healing. But Jesus singled out this particular woman.

Can you imagine what life had been like for this woman prior to her healing? I wonder how bent over she was. My back aches just thinking about it. Physical pain aside, what was it like to spend eighteen years facing downward, rather than straight ahead? To never look up to see a sunny sky? To be unable to look people in the eye? No doubt her stooped posture singled her out in a crowd. Chances are that probably wasn't a good thing, for the most part. Her literally downcast body language might have made it easy for people to dismiss her. But according to Jesus, the last shall be first in God's kingdom. And so it was for this woman.

Jesus called her to himself. That alone probably raised her stature, in her own eyes and that of others. He pronounced her free from that which oppressed her. Then he connected with her physically by placing his hands on her. Once touched by God, the woman stood up straight. She could finally look another person in the eye, and her first face-to-face encounter was with Jesus. That encounter freed her from years of bondage. No wonder she immediately began praising God!

How sad that the leader of the synagogue missed the joy and the power of that moment. His own vision was weighed down by the burden of keeping the letter of the Law. Jesus reminded him that people were permitted to work on the Sabbath to take care of their animals. He then pointed out that releasing a child of God from bondage was even more appropriate Sabbath work. This truth, however, did not lift the official's perspective, but put him and people like him "to shame." They missed their own opportunity to become free of the burden that held them down and blocked them from genuine worship.

In contrast, the woman, as a result of her experience, spontaneously praised God. What activity could be more proper on the Sabbath? Wasn't that the reason people came to places of worship?

WHAT WEIGHS US DOWN?

Jesus told the crowd that the woman had been bound by Satan and was now set free. Her stooped position was the result of bondage. What weighs us down? In the Book of Revelation, Satan is referred to as the "accuser" of believers (12:10). How easily we can be bent down under the burden of guilt over past mistakes. We all have regrets. We're all sinners. God knows that better than we do. Jesus knew Peter would deny him long before Peter did. That didn't stop Jesus from loving Peter or from choosing Peter to be the rock on which he built his church. The force that keeps us trapped in unrelenting remorse is not of God.

Whether or not we hang our heads, self-condemnation can't help but affect the way we interact with others. Unresolved guilt might keep us from standing up for ourselves in abusive situations; we may somehow feel we deserve it. It can keep us from taking a proactive stance for people or causes we care about because we fear we are worthless. It can hold us back from receiving the good God has in mind for us. It's the devil that tells us what we have done is unforgivable, not God. "God did not send the Son into the world to condemn the world, but in order that the world might be saved through him" (John 3:17). In our shame, we don't let our secrets see the light of day. If we avoid the sacrament of reconciliation or reject the power of forgiveness, we can't stand face-to-face with our fellow human beings.

Lingering guilt keeps us demoralized and in bondage to our human frailty.

This crippled woman's experience is a message of hope to us. We may not feel worthy to approach God because of our pasts. As he called the woman, Jesus is calling us. He wants us to come to him so he can free us from our burdens, no matter how long we've been carrying them. Once free, we, too, will be better able to praise God and share the good news with others who are burdened by their pasts.

PONDER

1. What do you think was most challenging about the woman's condition prior to her healing? Why?
2. What are some connections among physical posture, mental outlook, and spiritual awareness?
3. Once touched by Jesus, the woman was able to straighten up. What in you could be straightened by Jesus' touch?
4. What is the difference between guilt and shame?
5. How might praising God and standing up for ourselves be connected?

PRAY

Loving God, set me free from the shame and fear that cripple me, from the guilt and sorrow that weigh me down. Lift me up so that, strengthened by your touch, I can stand in the truth of your love.

The Man with Dropsy

Suffering Isn't Just about Me

On one occasion when Jesus was going to the house of a leader of the Pharisees to eat a meal on the sabbath, they were watching him closely. Just then, in front of him, there was a man who had dropsy. And Jesus asked the lawyers and Pharisees, "Is it lawful to cure people on the sabbath, or not?" But they were silent. So Jesus took him and healed him, and sent him away. Then he said to them, "If one of you has a child or an ox that has fallen into a well, will you not immediately pull it out on a sabbath day?" And they could not reply to this.

Luke 14:1–6

Dropsy is "a disease in which watery fluid collects in the body," according to the *Oxford American Dictionary*. In other words, as the Good News Translation of this passage says, the man's "legs and arms were swollen." Swelling can be incredibly painful. Imagine this man inching his way to Jesus, step after painful step. Did he realize that Pharisees and religious lawyers surrounded Jesus? Did he know it was the Sabbath, or did he not care?

We aren't told anything about this man. He might not have been a Jew, in which case he wouldn't have known the awkwardness of breaking the Sabbath law. He could have been a Jew so desperate for relief that the Sabbath law didn't matter to him. We don't know how the man ended up in his condition or what happened after he was healed. It's almost as if his healing is not the point of this passage at all. Of course his cure meant a great deal to him personally, but the story is not so much about him as about those religious experts who were watching.

A RECURRING THEME

This issue of healing on the Sabbath comes up time and again in stories of Jesus' healing. He consistently chose to alleviate suffering rather than uphold the letter of the Law. Wouldn't one example have been sufficient? In this age of mass media, information is literally at our fingertips day and night. One has to be proactive to avoid it. We have to remember that during the time of the Gospels, there was no mass communication. On a practical level, news of an incident in one remote village wouldn't necessarily or easily find its way to other communities. Challenges between Jesus and religious leaders probably played out anew in every town Jesus visited.

On the other hand, there are many recurring themes in Scripture. Gospel writers may have wanted to be sure that important messages weren't glossed over. We're used to hearing the stories about Jesus challenging scrupulosity in favor of compassion. We might find it difficult to sympathize with the scandal felt by the religious leaders. They were doing their sincere but mistaken best to live as they thought God wanted them to live. There are people today who feel guilty if they miss Mass on Sunday because of illness or hazardous weather. Our consciences sometimes grill us even when we've lost perspective.

So again, Jesus used this suffering man's condition as an opportunity to teach God's love. Compassion and service take precedence over keeping the law for the law's sake. This example can help us consider our own perspective regarding external observance versus a heart for God and his children.

CASE IN POINT

It's not that the man was not important or that his suffering didn't matter, but it suggests that sometimes our own suffering isn't solely about us. Our pain—and our recovery from it—can be about more than us. God can use our suffering to teach or to help others if we are willing to be used.

Plagued by swelling in his arms and legs, the man probably had difficulty using his arms to earn a living, help another person, or even give a hug. The pain of reaching might have curtailed his ability or his inclination to do so. Swollen legs would have made getting anywhere he wanted or needed to go difficult. It would have limited his sphere of functioning. Yet the man was willing to make the painful pilgrimage to Jesus. Once he encountered Jesus, presumably the swelling went down and his range of motion increased. Relieved of his pain, he was free to function more fully in his world.

HOW ARE WE SWOLLEN?

We no longer hear the term "dropsy." Modern medicine has treatment for any number of conditions that cause fluid buildup in various areas of the body. So what does this man's story have to do with us? What, within us, might be swollen? Maybe our egos are swollen. We may be so preoccupied with our own importance that we share our attention with others only with great difficulty. Self-centeredness doesn't always take the form of overblown pride. We can be filled—or even obsessed—with thoughts of our own inadequacies and problems. Our need to micromanage our little corner of the world might leave little room for thoughts of others. Our minds might be swollen with worries, distractions, or self-righteous criticism. Jesus will help shrink our overdeveloped preoccupations down to a healthy size, if we let him. We can disregard the Pharisee-like attitudes that tell us we need to be—or at least appear—good enough. Like the man with dropsy, we can come as we are. Persistence in spite of his painful journey demonstrated his faith that Jesus could do for him what he could not do for himself. Our journey to show ourselves as we truly are might be equally as painful, but it can also be equally rewarding.

PONDER

1. Jesus was on his way to share a meal with religious "success stories" when the man with dropsy approached him. What do you think enabled the man to approach Jesus in his state in front of such a crowd?
2. What, if any, are your scrupulous observances? Do they interfere with your ability to act in love? Why or why not?
3. Name some ways our culture makes it easy for us to become swollen with pride.
4. What are the things within you that crowd out your ability to relate to the world around you?

PRAY

Divine Healer, when my mind is swollen with pride or self-centered worry, restore my overdeveloped ego to its proper size.

20

Ten Lepers Healed

Skin-Deep Healing and More

On the way to Jerusalem Jesus was going through the region between Samaria and Galilee. As he entered a village, ten lepers approached him. Keeping their distance, they called out, saying, "Jesus, Master, have mercy on us!" When he saw them, he said to them, "Go and show yourselves to the priests." And as they went, they were made clean. Then one of them, when he saw that he was healed, turned back, praising God with a loud voice. He prostrated himself at Jesus' feet and thanked him. And he was a Samaritan. Then Jesus asked, "Were not ten made clean? But the other nine, where are they? Was none of them found to return and give praise to God except this foreigner?" Then he said to him, "Get up and go on your way; your faith has made you well."

Luke 17:11–19

Why did Jesus ask where the other nine were? They were doing what Jesus had told them to do. He told them to present themselves to the priests, and that's what they did. The procedure for healing skin diseases according to Jewish law included examination by the priests. It also involved a number of offerings to be sacrificed (see Lev 14:1–32). Compliance with this ritual and making the prescribed offerings would not only signify healing but presumably include praise and thanksgiving to God, as well. It seems as if Jesus didn't expect more until he witnessed it from an unexpected source.

The nine were obedient to Jesus' instructions and to the Jewish law. In contrast, the Samaritan, on his way to performing the ritual, realized that God's power had already healed him. Caught up in spontaneous joy, the man could not contain himself. He did an about-face, retraced his steps, and threw himself at Jesus' feet in gratitude. On the way, he praised God. The Samaritan's joy bubbled over into praise and gratitude. Through direct contact with Jesus and his own response, he achieved what the Jewish ritual had been designed to do. He experienced healing and gave glory to God.

OUTSIDE THE BOX

Maybe it was easier for this Samaritan to return to Jesus instead of heading straight to the priests. He was, after all, a foreigner, not as bound to the Jewish law as the other nine might have been. But he lived out what the law was designed to signify externally. After this demonstration of dynamic faith, Jesus didn't tell him he still had to go back and show himself to the priests. He told the man to go on his way.

In a larger sense, the Samaritan did present himself to a "priest." Jesus is a priest like Melchizedek, made a priest not by human rules and regulations but by the power of eternal life. The old rule was to be set aside because Jesus provided a better hope (see Heb 7:15–19). The Samaritan, not as closely tied to Jewish regulations, was able to tap into this better hope and at the same time give thanks to God in the person of Jesus.

After Jesus acknowledged the Samaritan's gratitude, he told him he could get up (from the prostrated position of humility he had assumed) and go on his way. His "way" was presumably a return to his native area, Samaria, where worship was not centered on the temple in Jerusalem.

Jesus also said to him, "Your faith has made you well." All ten were made clean, that is, healed of leprosy. Only one was pronounced "well." Being disease-free and having a state of well-being are not the same thing.

Jesus didn't come to do away with the law but rather to empower its teachings to become possible (see Matt 5:17). The experience of the Samaritan in light of the behavior of the other nine lepers models this phenomenon. The nine followed the prescriptions of the law as directed by Jesus. They were relieved of their leprosy. But the prescribed healing process may have only been skin-deep, literally. Somehow it didn't seem to have the transformative power that the Samaritan experienced within his heart. He responded accordingly, following the conversion of his spirit rather than an external precept. As a result, the Samaritan was not only relieved of his malady, but made well, that is, made whole in body, mind, and spirit.

SURRENDERING OURSELVES

It may have been easier for a foreigner who grew up without the constraints of Jewish law to respond freely to the miracle. Some of us aren't used to thinking "outside the box" of orthodox religious practices. We may overlook opportunities for true conversion of our hearts when they happen. We may even fear experiences that call us out of our comfort zones and the security of religious routine. Despite our devotion and reverence for God, we may find ourselves reciting prayers by rote, or repeating automatically the responses during church services.

We can miss the power that the words and rituals convey. We cheat ourselves of dynamic spiritual experience.

That's not to say that we'll have emotionally laden highs during every Mass or prayer time. We probably won't. Many saints experienced periods of dryness and dark nights but persevered on their faith journeys. When we feel far away from God because of distress or apathy, we can still call out to God, just as the ten lepers called out to Jesus from a distance. They weren't close to him, but that didn't prevent his healing power from reaching them.

When we do call out, we can pray for awareness. The Samaritan noticed that he had been healed on his way to the priest. All ten lepers were made clean on the way to the priest, but the Gospel says that the one who came back to Jesus did so when he saw that he was clean. Maybe the others didn't notice they were clean or didn't look for a change until they arrived at their destination. We can pray to be mindful, to notice when our prayers are answered. We need to be open to the unexpected ways God may answer those prayers. With increased awareness, we may find many more things to be grateful for. Then we can continue on our way, like the Samaritan, praising God and experiencing a deeper sense of wellness than we might otherwise know.

PONDER

1. What is the difference between religious observance and allowing the power of God to impact your life?
2. What are some things that can block God's power from changing your heart?
3. In what ways have you experienced healing in your life?

4. In what ways would you like to experience a deeper sense of well-being?
5. The lepers called out to Jesus from a distance. When have you felt far away from God but still called out to him? What happened?

PRAY

Lord of all Creation, you are not limited by my assumptions. Open my mind and heart to notice your healing power, even when it comes in unexpected ways. Lead me to a deeper sense of well-being based on your presence, not my frailty.

21

The Official's Son

Our Ways Are Not God's Ways

Then [Jesus] came again to Cana in Galilee where he had changed the water into wine. Now there was a royal official whose son lay ill in Capernaum. When he heard that Jesus had come from Judea to Galilee, he went and begged him to come down and heal his son, for he was at the point of death. Then Jesus said to him, "Unless you see signs and wonders you will not believe."

The official said to him, "Sir, come down before my little boy dies." Jesus said to him, "Go; your son will live." The man believed the word that Jesus spoke to him and started on his way. As he was going down, his slaves met him and told him that his child was alive. So he asked them the hour when he began to recover, and they said to him, "Yesterday at one in the afternoon the fever left him." The father realized that this was the hour when Jesus had said to him, "Your son will live." So he himself believed, along with his whole household.

John 4:46–53

Because his son's life was at stake, a royal official was willing to beg for Jesus' help. People in positions of power are used to having things done for them. Out of love for his son, this administrator willingly humbled himself before Jesus, a member of the fringe element. The official's clout did him no good in his current need. All this man's status, influence, and money couldn't save his son. In this situation, he saw that Jesus' reputed power was considerably more than his own. Love kept the man from being too proud to ask for help.

This desperate father was in no position to demand anything. He came to Jesus with humility, an essential attitude when approaching God. That's not because God needs or wants kowtowing; it's just an accurate perception of reality. Our loving God is also the all-powerful and supreme Creator.

Nevertheless, Jesus seemed frustrated or at least disappointed that the people in general, and this official in particular, had trouble trusting him. The man not only asked for Jesus to heal the boy but also told Jesus how to go about it. He wanted Jesus to "come down and heal his son." It was a subtle instruction, but an instruction nonetheless. The man wanted Jesus to travel from Cana to Capernaum to heal the boy in person. It seems like a reasonable expectation, but when we expect God to do things the way we think God should, we may be in for surprises.

After Jesus expressed his exasperation, the man repeated himself: "Sir, come down before my little boy dies." Jesus told the man to go home; his son would live. Although Jesus accompanied Jairus to his home to heal his dying little daughter, Jesus chose not to go with this official. Even so, his mercy extended to both children. Why a different method for two apparently similar situations? God alone knows the reason. Perhaps the differences are not evident from our limited viewpoint.

For whatever reason, Jesus had this father return home on his own, after reassuring him that the boy would live. Maybe sending him home unaccompanied was an opportunity for the man to act on faith he didn't know he had. Heading home alone was a practical demonstration of obedient trust in Jesus. That trust was not misplaced. En route, the official's servants met him with good news: his son was alive and had improved at the exact time that Jesus affirmed the boy's recovery. Eventually the official's entire household was convinced, but his own journey of faith began with his first step toward home.

TRUST AND OPEN-MINDEDNESS

"Seeing is believing," says an old maxim. We may have said it ourselves. That's not a bad motto when looking for results from material goods or even when developing trust in our relationships with other fallible human beings. But we're called to an entirely different level of trust in relation to God. God doesn't owe us proof of anything. Nevertheless, God provides all that we need and continues to invite us into ever-deepening levels of trust in God. It may be a long, slow process. That's okay. God is well aware of both our potential and our human frailty.

For example, although we may pray sincerely on behalf of our loved ones or about a particular dilemma, we may have expectations. When that's the case, we watch for answers to come in the way we think they should. But our ways are not God's ways. Just because a situation doesn't go the way we think it should, doesn't mean its outcome can't be good. We may pray for a problem to be resolved, and when it isn't, we may feel that God has turned his back on us. We may not be aware of the benefits of working through or enduring the problem while we're still in the situation. The struggle may have strengthened our character in some way. It may have taught us patience or compassion.

Our expectations don't limit God; they only limit our trust in God. When faced with a hungry crowd of five thousand, the apostles expected Jesus to solve the problem by sending the people away to fend for themselves. Jesus had another solution in mind. Let's not stare so long at the door we want to open that we miss another door when it opens.

PONDER

1. In desperation, the official asked Jesus to come with him and heal his son. Jesus answered the man's deeper request for healing without doing what the man expected. What do you think gave the man the courage to head for home without Jesus?

2. Jesus said that unless we see signs and wonders, we will not believe. Have you seen signs and wonders in your own life? How and when did you become aware of them?

3. When have your expectations limited your ability to find joy?

4. After the boy was healed, the official's entire family believed, even though they had not encountered Jesus directly. How can one person's faith experience impact others? How can your own faith experience influence those you come in contact with?

PRAY

All-knowing God, help me trust that you know better than I do. Remind me that things can work out for the best even when they don't go the way I think they should.

22

The Man Born Blind

Darkest before the Dawn

As [Jesus] walked along, he saw a man blind from birth. His disciples asked him, "Rabbi, who sinned, this man or his parents, that he was born blind?" Jesus answered, "Neither this man nor his parents sinned; he was born blind so that God's works might be revealed in him. We must work the works of him who sent me while it is day; night is coming when no one can work. As long as I am in the world, I am the light of the world." When he had said this, he spat on the ground and made mud with the saliva and spread the mud on the man's eyes, saying to him, "Go, wash in the pool of Siloam" (which means Sent). Then he went and washed and came back able to see. The neighbors and those who had seen him before as a beggar began to ask, "Is this not the man who used to sit and beg?" Some were saying, "It is he." Others were saying, "No, but it is someone like him." He kept saying, "I am the man." But they kept asking him, "Then how were your eyes opened?" He answered, "The man called Jesus made mud, spread it on my eyes, and said to me, 'Go to Siloam and wash.' Then I went and washed and

received my sight." They said to him, "Where is he?"
He said, "I do not know."

John 9:1–12

Jesus saw the man born blind, as did his disciples. The disciples concluded that the man's blindness was the result of sin. In that culture, afflictions were thought to be punishment for sin. Still, it seems shortsighted for them to wonder if the man's own sin had caused his blindness. He had been blind since birth. How could he possibly have been guilty of sin before he was born? At least the disciples allowed the possibility that his affliction might have been the result of his parents' sin.

Jesus assured his disciples that the man's blindness was not a punishment for anyone's sin but an opportunity for God's power to be revealed. After identifying himself as "the light of the world," Jesus blocked the man's vision even more. He made mud by spitting in the dirt and spread the mud over the blind man's eyes. Sometimes it really is darkest before the dawn. One would think that healing would involve removing obstacles from the man's vision, not adding more. Now, mud covered the man's eyes, but the process didn't end there. Jesus sent the man to wash away the mud. Not just to wipe it with a towel, or splash water on his face, but to wash in a specific pool, the name of which meant "Sent." The man obeyed and was able to see. In dealing with the additional problem of mud on his eyes, the underlying cause of the man's blindness was healed.

MORE THAN MEETS THE EYE

So often, things have to get worse before they get better. In our times of darkness, we may not be able to see how God can help. We blindly grope for solutions that don't come. We want to see the answers before we let go of our control. We don't understand that our own lack of vision can prevent us from finding the solutions we seek. Sometimes only a turn for the worse makes us willing.

It would never have occurred to the blind man to go to the pool of Siloam until Jesus gave him a reason to wash and then "sent" him. Although Jesus' action restored the man's sight, the man also had to participate in his healing by following instructions.

While we can't always heal ourselves, there are things we need to do to cooperate with the healing process. We may need outside help but be reluctant to pursue it because we think things aren't that bad. We procrastinate or devote ourselves to other priorities. Then the crisis comes—a heart attack, a serious rift in our marriage, a drunk-driving arrest. We may be more willing to seek help once the situation worsens. We go to the doctor or the marriage counselor or the support group. They can help, but only to the extent that we follow their instructions.

We may need to take actions that will not only help us through the immediate crisis but also address the underlying causes. The heart-attack patient has to adjust his diet and begin a reasonable exercise regimen. Marriage counseling may involve each spouse working on his or her individual issues before each can relate to the other in a healthier way. The addict may find that there is a lot more to recovery than simply not picking up the drug. In order to benefit from healing opportunities, we need to do our part. We can't do it alone, but we can't be passive recipients, either. Healing may well be a gift, but we must unwrap the gift and use it.

BLINDED IN SPITE OF THE LIGHT

The man born blind was not the only one who couldn't see. Jesus, "the light of the world," was the only one in the story who saw with clarity. He saw that there was more to the blind man than his disability. The apostles initially couldn't see past the attitude that the unfortunate somehow deserve their misfortune. That attitude leaves little room for compassion. The people who had seen the blind man previously couldn't see past his disability. They pegged him as a blind beggar. Once he could see and move independently, they wondered if it was the same man. It's as if his identity was his blindness. Once that identity was taken away, people didn't recognize him. It's almost heartbreaking that he had to keep saying that he really was the same person.

THE ROCKY ROAD TO RECOVERY

Once healed, this man's life wasn't carefree. John's Gospel goes on to tell us that the man was brought to the Jewish religious leaders for questioning. He had been healed on a Sabbath, which broke the Sabbath law of rest. When he told them how Jesus healed him, the Pharisees didn't believe the man. They even called in his parents to verify he'd been blind from birth. His parents, apparently afraid of being barred from the synagogue, refused to get involved.

The Pharisees claimed that Jesus was a sinner. Initially, the healed man didn't know (and may not have cared) if Jesus was a sinner or not. The religious leaders, clinging to their traditions and legalistic interpretation of the law, refused to see the larger truth. They continued to challenge the man. His own experience convinced him that whatever power Jesus had must have come from God. As the man told the Pharisees, "We know that God does not listen to sinners....If this man were not from God, he could do nothing" (John 9:31, 33). At that point the leaders expelled him from the synagogue.

The man had been doubted by the people in his daily life, abandoned by his parents, and thrown out of the synagogue. He was on his own. That's when Jesus came to him again. Jesus offered this totally isolated man the only thing that Jesus had left to offer him. Jesus asked him if he believed "in the Son of Man." With his former support network pulled out from under him, the man was open and willing to take his relationship with Jesus to the next level. When Jesus identified himself as Lord, the man believed and worshipped Jesus (see John 9:13–38).

GRADUALLY INCREASING LIGHT

When asked immediately after his healing, the man didn't know where or even who Jesus was. As the Pharisees probed, the man's understanding of Jesus developed. He concluded Jesus could *not* be a sinner but must be of God. When he encountered Jesus a second time, the man was prepared to accept Jesus as his Lord and Messiah. Although the man's physical blindness was healed in a single instant when he washed, his spiritual vision, his awareness of who Jesus was and understanding of their relationship, continued to evolve.

Healing seemed to make things worse instead of better. Sometimes it may seem like that to us, too. The heart-attack victim doesn't like doing without the rich foods or getting off the comfortable sofa to exercise. The troubled couple may not like the soul-searching involved in uncovering how their own personality flaws contribute to their marital conflict. The addict may miss his old haunts and the familiar faces of his drinking buddies. But if these people persist on their new paths, their lives will continue to change for the better. The temporary discomfort will be worth the benefits. Similarly, if we continue doing our best to follow where we believe Jesus is "sending" us, if we persist even when we feel abandoned or challenged by those we love, we will be rewarded. Increasing light will clarify who we are, who God is, and how we fit in with God's plan.

PONDER

1. Have you heard people say that certain people "deserve" what they're suffering? What do you think lies behind a "blame the victim" attitude?

2. People who knew the blind man had trouble recognizing the healed man as the same person. What are some ways to see people as more than their challenges or disabilities?

3. In spite of the doubts and questions thrown at him, the healed man was unshaken because of his direct experience with the truth. When has your own experience strengthened you to stand up to challenges?

4. The man's understanding of who Jesus was gradually developed. How has your understanding of who Jesus is grown over time?

5. Although Jesus healed the man by putting mud on his eyes, the man had to do his part by following instructions and washing. What in you needs healing? What is your part in cooperating with the healing you seek?

PRAY

Jesus, Light of the World, sometimes it's darkest before the dawn. Help me cooperate with the healing process as I place my trust in you.

23

Malchus, the High Priest's Slave

In the Heat of the Moment

While [Jesus] was still speaking, suddenly a crowd came, and the one called Judas, one of the twelve, was leading them. He approached Jesus to kiss him; but Jesus said to him, "Judas is it with a kiss that you are betraying the Son of Man?" When those who were around him saw what was coming, they asked, "Lord, should we strike with the sword?" Then one of them struck the slave of the high priest and cut off his right ear. But Jesus said, "No more of this!" And he touched his ear and healed him.

Luke 22:47–51

Then Simon Peter, who had a sword, drew it, struck the high priest's slave, and cut off his right ear. The slave's name was Malchus.

John 18:10

Sent by the chief priests, a mob of soldiers and police surrounded Jesus to arrest him. Fight-or-flight mode probably kicked in for Peter, and he lashed out. As a result, Malchus, the high priest's slave, lost an ear.

Why Malchus? Was he somehow more threatening than armed soldiers? More likely, he just happened to be standing in the wrong place—an arm's length away from panicky Peter—at the wrong time. Maybe Malchus genuinely thought Jesus was a blasphemer worthy of imprisonment. Maybe he was just following orders. He was, after all, only a slave.

In a bold but ineffective move, Peter cut off the slave's ear. In a flash, Malchus went from the sidelines into the middle of the drama. He probably reeled from the pain and shock of the brutal attack. He could hardly have expected violence from a follower of Jesus who taught, "Blessed are the peacemakers."

Peter meant well. Maybe he felt a particular need to demonstrate his loyalty. Jesus had predicted that Peter would deny him before the night was over. But Peter's desperate attempt to help only made matters worse. There stood Malchus with a gaping wound in the side of his head.

Jesus put a stop to the violence. He not only told his followers to cease and desist, he undid the harm caused by Peter's rash action. Jesus touched Malchus's ear and healed him.

Jesus had just been tormented by the personal agony he endured while his nearest and dearest followers slept. He worked his way through accepting the violent events he knew were about to unfold. He was concerned about not losing "a single one of those" his Father had given him (John 18:9). He faced an angry gang of armed soldiers. Any one of these things could have demanded Jesus' full attention. Yet he healed his enemy's slave.

Maybe Malchus secretly sympathized with Jesus. Maybe, like his master, Malchus condemned Jesus. It didn't seem to matter. Jesus healed him anyway. Once healed, it seems unlikely that a hardened attitude toward Jesus could have remained unchanged. Jesus often told people, "Listen, then, if you have ears to hear."

Jesus had literally given Malchus an ear with which to receive the truth.

CAN WE IDENTIFY?

At different points in our lives, we may identify in some way with most of the people involved in this story. Like the soldiers and police, we may use whatever authority or force we have to maintain order in our lives. When we're afraid, we try to impose our vision of what's right on others. The religious leaders sent others to arrest Jesus while they waited securely in their headquarters. Avoiding direct conflict, we may manipulate or send others to fight our battles while we remain safely detached.

There may be times when we relate to Peter. We sense danger. We feel threatened by forces beyond our control. We feel driven to do something, anything, to quell our fear. So we act impulsively, without any clear sense of why or what we hope to achieve. We just want to relieve the tension within ourselves by taking action.

Sometimes we barely feel able to cope with our own inner turmoil or conflicts with others. Thinking about what our opponents may be going through seems like more than we can manage. In the heat of the moment, it may be unrealistic to expect ourselves to act with the grace that Jesus showed. Still, what a model this is to think about.

Jesus reached out to undo the harm Peter caused to the injured slave. If we have ever been on the receiving end of a sincere apology from someone who has hurt us, we know its healing power. Extending our own sincere apologies and appropriate changes in behavior, we can do the same. Even if our apology is not accepted, reaching out has healing power. Unlike Jesus, who did not need healing of his own heart, we may have yet to experience the peace of extending our hands to heal the hurts our words or actions have caused. Once healed, maybe Malchus himself became more conscious of how he treated those who opposed him or treated him unfairly. May God's healing touch open the ears of our hearts to a new attitude toward those who disagree with us.

PONDER

1. Malchus was with those who went to arrest Jesus. Maybe he believed in what he was doing or maybe he was just following orders. What bearing do you think his motivation had on the events that unfolded?
2. Peter reacted to a threatening situation by lashing out. What prompts you to lash out at others? What might help you handle those situations in a different way?
3. How do you think Malchus felt when he realized he'd been attacked? How do you think his reaction changed when Jesus healed the wound?
4. Have you ever been on the receiving end of a heartfelt apology from someone who hurt you? How did it feel? How might that experience make it easier for you to make amends for the hurts you've caused others?
5. When might it not be wise or appropriate to make amends to people you've hurt in the past?

PRAY

Prince of Peace, it's easy to lash out when I feel threatened. Teach my heart to treat with patience and respect those who oppose me.

24

The Cruel Centurion

Penetrating a Hardened Heart

Then the soldiers of the governor took Jesus into the governor's headquarters, and they gathered the whole cohort around him. They stripped him and put a scarlet robe on him, and after twisting some thorns into a crown, they put it on his head. They put a reed in his right hand and knelt before him and mocked him, saying, "Hail, King of the Jews!" They spat on him, and took the reed and struck him on the head. After mocking him, they stripped him of the robe and put his own clothes on him. Then they led him away to crucify him....And when they had crucified him, they divided his clothes among themselves by casting lots; then they sat down there and kept watch over him.

Matthew 27:27–31; 35–36

It was now about noon, and darkness came over the whole land until three in the afternoon, while the sun's light failed; and the curtain of the temple was torn in two. Then Jesus, crying with a loud voice, said, "Father, into your hands I commend my spirit." Having said this, he breathed his last. When the cen-

turion saw what had taken place, he praised God and
said, "Certainly this man was innocent."

Luke 23:44–47

The centurion in charge of the execution had probably supervised
the execution of countless prisoners. Torture was a routine part of
the job. The soldiers under him who led Jesus away to be crucified had entertained themselves with mocking and cruelty at
Jesus' expense. Indifferent to his suffering during his agonizing
death, they focused on their own gain and gambled for his
clothes. Matthew's account of the crucifixion includes a descrip-
tion of an earthquake at the time of Jesus' death (see 27:51–54).
Luke's version above, however, suggests that the centurion's
response was not the result of a cataclysmic natural event. If ter-
ror alone caused the centurion's response, if he feared for his own
safety in light of his role in Jesus' death, he might have run away,
or lashed out in defiant defense of his responsibility in the matter. He might have collapsed in sobs of regret and pleas for mercy.
Instead, he praised God and spoke the truth. He testified to the
good news: Jesus was the innocent, holy Son of God. Did his
response have less to do with the earthquake and more to do with
what he had observed of Jesus' response to insults and suffering?

Those in charge of watching over Jesus during his crucifixion had a lot to observe. The soldiers' cruelty didn't take away
Jesus' dignity, only their own. Jesus didn't cower or lash out in
response to brutality. He expressed his pain, but he did so without recrimination. Rather, he prayed that his persecutors be forgiven. Although he cried out from the cross, "My God, my God,
why have you forsaken me?" (Matt 27:46), he resolutely entrusted
his spirit with his last breath to that same God.

PENETRATING A HARDENED HEART

Although the centurion had witnessed countless beatings, tortures, and executions, no doubt he had never witnessed someone respond in such a way as Jesus. It may not have taken an earthquake for this centurion to recognize holiness when he saw it. Jesus reflected God's incredible love, not only with his life, but also with his dying moments. Betrayal, humiliation, physical pain: none of these could take away Jesus' free will, his choice to remain faithful to his heavenly Father. They couldn't prevent him from continuing to love and forgive.

The centurion's heart, calloused by countless examples of "man's inhumanity to man" as a way of life, was touched, softened, and quite possibly healed, by Jesus' quiet refusal to respond in kind. Even under the dire circumstances, grace melted the hardened heart enough to allow love to enter and bring forth praise. One has to wonder what the centurion did with the rest of his life following that moment of grace.

WE ALWAYS HAVE CHOICES

Even when our freedom seems limited, we always have choices. Jesus didn't have to come down from the cross or change his circumstances to touch others. He fulfilled God's purpose for him even though he didn't change events as they unfolded. This can encourage us when we find ourselves drawn into circumstances beyond our power to control. We can't always change situations; we certainly can't change other people. But we can always choose how we respond. Our responses, limited as they may seem to us, and even to others, can speak volumes. They reveal who we are, who God is in our lives and who God can be in the lives of those around us.

We may not be able to fully live up to Jesus' example of unwavering grace and perfect forgiveness for those who hurt us or remain indifferent to our suffering. Chances are we don't always have unfailing concern for others when we ourselves are in pain. We can take heart. If Jesus prayed for and forgave his persecutors, his compassion will certainly extend to us in our struggles.

We might find ourselves hardened by what we've seen of needless suffering and senseless cruelty in the world. We might even find ourselves contributing to it—perhaps not by overt cruelty, but by silently standing by rather than speaking out. If we do, we don't have to get caught up in remorse and turn our thoughts inward. Like the centurion, we can keep watch over those in our world who are rising above a culture preoccupied with self-centeredness, greed, and the like. We can lift our minds and hearts to praise God who is bigger than all the cruelty in the world. We can take inspiration from those who light candles in the darkness. We can join our lights—however small they seem to be—to the Light that all the darkness in the world can never put out (see John 1:5).

PONDER

1. It's easy to judge the soldiers who amused themselves at Jesus' expense. What are some of the things that enable people to become indifferent to the suffering of others?

2. The centurion became convinced that Jesus was the Son of God because of what he saw. What have you seen that convinces you that Jesus is the Son of God?

3. The centurion saw the events that took place because he was keeping watch. How are you keeping watch in your life today? Is there something in your life you are feeling called to watch more closely?

4. Rather than become immobilized by fear or overwhelmed by guilt when he realized that he had executed the Son of God, the centurion praised God in awe. Why do you think he was able to do that? How can you choose to praise God in the face of your own fear or guilt?

PRAY

When what I've seen of suffering and cruelty overwhelms me, Lord, remind me that your love is bigger than all the pain and sorrow in the world.

25

Peter

The Healing of Guilt

[Jesus said], "Simon, Simon, listen! Satan has demanded to sift all of you like wheat, but I have prayed for you that your own faith may not fail; and you, when once you have turned back, strengthen your brothers." And he said to him, "Lord, I am ready to go with you to prison and to death!" Jesus said, "I tell you, Peter, the cock will not crow this day, until you have denied three times that you know me."

Luke 22:31–34

Then a servant-girl, seeing [Peter] in the firelight, stared at him and said, "This man also was with [Jesus]. But he denied it, saying, "Woman, I do not know him." A little later someone else, on seeing him, said, "You also are one of them." But Peter said, "Man, I am not!" Then about an hour later still another kept insisting, "Surely this man also was with him; for he is a Galilean." But Peter said, "Man, I do not know what you are talking about!" At that moment, while he was still speaking, the cock crowed. The Lord turned and looked at Peter... and [Peter] went out and wept bitterly.

Luke 22:56–62

When they had finished breakfast, [the resurrected] Jesus said to Simon Peter, "Simon son of John, do you love me more than these?" He said to him, "Yes, Lord; you know that I love you." Jesus said to him, "Feed my lambs." A second time he said to him, "Simon son of John, do you love me?" He said to him, "Yes, Lord; you know that I love you." Jesus said to him, "Tend my sheep." He said to him the third time, "Simon son of John, do you love me?" Peter felt hurt because he said to him the third time, "Do you love me?" And he said to him, "Lord, you know everything; you know that I love you." Jesus said to him, "Feed my sheep. Very truly, I tell you, when you were younger, you used to fasten your own belt and to go wherever you wished. But when you grow old, you will stretch out your hands, and someone else will fasten a belt around you and take you where you do not wish to go." (He said this to indicate that kind of death by which he would glorify God.) After this he said to [Peter], "Follow me."

John 21:15–19

Peter, the rock on which Jesus built his church, was utterly human. When Jesus first called him, Peter told Jesus to depart from him because he was a sinful man (see Luke 5:8). Peter had a gut-level awareness of his human weaknesses. By the time he had followed Jesus for three years, Peter seemed to have forgotten his imperfections. Maybe he felt he had grown beyond his early days as a sinner. Maybe he had. But he had not outgrown human frailty. Jesus was well aware of Peter's weaknesses, but loved him and chose him anyway.

After Jesus was taken prisoner by the Jewish authorities, Peter denied Jesus three times, as predicted. Peter's failure is well recorded in the Gospels. Only Peter and one other disciple, however, even dared enter the "enemy territory" of the high priest's house. The other apostles were nowhere to be found.

When first accused of being Jesus' disciple, Peter denied it. He could have made himself scarce at that point, but he remained. That seems to indicate some degree of loyalty and concern for Jesus. It was not until the cock crowed that Peter's awareness of his own cowardice crashed in on him. Overcome with sorrow, Peter left.

COURAGE TO CONTINUE

Peter could have been crippled easily by the burden of his guilt. He not only denied Jesus, but he failed to live up to his own expectations of himself. Peter abandoned Jesus after boasting undying loyalty. Despair could have led him to commit suicide, as Judas did. He could have avoided the other apostles out of shame, but that's not what happened. Peter wept bitterly, but somehow found the willingness and humility to rejoin the other apostles at some point during Jesus' trial, crucifixion, and death. When the risen Christ appeared to the apostles, Peter was right there with them.

How did Peter find the courage to face the others after abandoning Jesus in spite of his boast of unwavering faithfulness? Perhaps Peter's healing of guilt began as he remembered that Jesus not only predicted his denial but also assured Peter he had prayed for him. More than that, Jesus told Peter there was a job for him to do after he turned back. Jesus wanted Peter to "strengthen" his brothers. He could encourage the others—not because Peter had been a tower of strength—but because he had been all too human. The apostles could relate to Peter. Therefore, they didn't have to be eaten alive by guilt or shame.

When the resurrected Jesus appeared to the apostles, he wished them all peace. He later, however, invited Peter to make three affirmations of love, counteracting his three denials. It saddened Peter to hear Jesus ask three times, but perhaps Jesus knew it was something Peter needed to do for his own sake. With each affirmation, Peter was recommissioned to feed the Lord's sheep. This made it clear that Peter could best show his love for Jesus, not by changing the past, but by acting in the present with love. Peter's love for Jesus could best be shown by taking care of the others that Jesus loved.

OUR OWN FLAWED FAITHFULNESS

Like Peter, as we answer Jesus' call, some of us have a sense of our own inadequacies. Others, perhaps blessed with some spiritual growth, might be lulled into complacency or be tempted by self-righteousness. We may feel surprised or guilt-ridden when we lose our tempers or catch ourselves failing to live up to our ideals. Might that be pride in disguise? Is it really so surprising that we aren't perfect? People who appear perfect can be intimidating. Sometimes when we allow others to see our imperfections, we become approachable and better able to serve them.

When we face our flaws and share them with God and with another trusted person, such as we do in the sacrament of reconciliation, we grow spiritually. These are graced opportunities. We don't condemn ourselves but accept God's glorious mercy and the healing love of forgiveness. When we have received forgiveness as pure gift, we can extend that same gift to others. It is easy to be critical when we seem to be doing things right, when we compare ourselves to others and appear to come out ahead. On the other hand, we might compare ourselves to others and decide we don't measure up or that we're too flawed to be used by God. Both are counterproductive.

If we want a gauge of how faithful to Christ we are, Christ's interaction with Peter gives us a great tool. Are we feeding his sheep? Are we taking care of the ones he loves? What we do to the least of them, we do to him.

PONDER

1. Why do you suppose Peter felt he would be able to remain faithful to Jesus throughout Jesus' trial and persecution? What do you think was behind his bold statement of loyalty?
2. Have you ever found yourself unable to live up to your own expectations? What happened?
3. What is the biggest challenge in accepting forgiveness as a free gift, rather than something you deserve or have to earn?
4. Do you suppose Jesus forgave Peter before or after he told Peter to feed his sheep three times? What is the relationship between penance, making amends, and mercy?

PRAY

Loving Savior, grant me the courage to face my own weaknesses. Help me accept the healing power of your forgiveness. Teach me to forgive myself.